Advance Praise for Wi

"Rob Wilson is among those courage to be vulnerable in and often funny stories he shares from his own life experiences will have you feeling like you are hanging out with your wisest friend having a heart to heart conversation. It is wonderful to know I can tap into this source of inspiration and encouragement anytime I need a boost." **Patty Kitching**, President, Speaking For You

"Rob Wilson uses his life experiences and keen perceptions to entertain and motivate his audiences, whether in person or in print. He captures your attention -- and even your heart -- through his excellent storytelling. It's a fun and relaxing adventure each time he shares a story. You don't want to miss a word." **Don Gammill**, Communities Editor, *The Oklahoman*

"Wisdom in the Weirdest Places is witty, thought-provoking, sometimes hilarious and sometimes embarrassingly honest. It's a refreshing change from many of the business books I've read - stories about people who survive and thrive. Rob's real-life experiences will motivate and prod you into seeing the opportunity for positive change in every corner of your life while your spirits are lifted." **Sheila Fredrickson**, Editor, *ProService Magazine*, National Electronics Service Dealers Association, and Author, *Only In Church: Hysterically Funny Church Stories*

"Rob Wilson has a great talent for inspiring others with his down to earth stories of real folks. Over a period of several years I used Rob's monthly writings consistently to inspire and motivate my sales staff. His ability to turn stories of life events into lessons of forgiveness, confidence or perseverance had my staff looking forward to his lesson each month and left them feeling good about themselves and mankind." **John Boggs**, Author, *ADvice by John Boggs - Common Sense Stories of Local Advertising and Sales*

"*Wisdom in the Weirdest Places* is a revealing and insightful collection of stories on motivation. It should be read by anyone who spends time trying to motivate those around them or who may be aspiring to be a true leader. Anything Rob Wilson has to say about motivation is worth listening to – several times over." **Bill Smith**, Editor, *Commonwealth Chief*, Virginia Fire Chiefs Association.

"The introspective yet outward-looking feature column, *The Un-Comfort Zone*, has inspired a large Toronto readership for years as Robert Evans Wilson, Jr. shares his unique understanding of life and living. A thoughtful and creative writer, Rob finds his inspiration in the very moments that embarrass or challenge many of us. He presents real-life solutions from his own experiences or those others share with him, detailing in simple language the resolution of conflicts with upbeat and insightful commentary." **Frank Touby**, Editor-in-Chief, *The Bulletin* in Toronto, Canada

"With a great deal of practicality, a lot of humor and an incredible insight, Rob Wilson, writes from the soul about life's lessons learned and new ones to explore. Read his writing and be uplifted!" **Jan Waggoner**, Publisher, *Living With Loss Magazine*

"Rob Wilson has hit upon something in his articles of wisdom. They not only cause you to think, they cause and encourage you to think about the way you think. When that occurs, you have a winner worth reading and treasuring. Thinking is good; thinking about the way you think is outstanding!" **Jim "Gymbeaux" Brown**, Author, *Nuggets For The Noggin* and *Real Estate Lagniappe*

"Rob's book, *Wisdom in the Weirdest Places*, is aptly named. He has a knack for taking everyday, ordinary events, and gleaning valuable life lessons from them. It's a good read that I highly recommend." **Rich Vurva**, Editor, *Industrial Supply Magazine*

"Our subscribers thoroughly enjoy Robert's articles which offer practical advice using down-to-earth examples anyone can relate to. Robert's keen insight allows him to use every day events to teach readers about motivation, empowerment, overcoming adversity, and several other inspiring topics." **Veronica I. "Ronnie" Jones**, Managing Publisher, *WorldWide Drilling Resource* magazine

"Rob Wilson's book *Wisdom in the Weirdest Places* is fantastic not only because of his perspective on his experiences and the motivation and moral he takes from each one, but how he shows us they can apply to our lives as well. I have found his vignettes to be funny, thought-provoking, and helpful not only in my every day challenges but in the overall fabric of my life. Rob believes in storytelling as an illustrative exercise that can carry us on a journey of introspection and discovery that makes us all feel good about ourselves." **Linda Kotrba**, Editor, *SutureLine*, magazine of the American Association of Surgical Physician Assistants

"I find Rob's stories to be inspiring. The way he talks about his life experiences keeps the reader fascinated. There seems to be a message for everyone." **Diana Curran**, Editor, *The Merchant Magazine*, Maryland Retailers Association

"Robert Wilson's syndicated column, *The Un-Comfort Zone*, has been published for several years as a featured column in our local section newsletter. His story fashion of conveying motivational concepts has been well-received. Now in book format as *Wisdom in the Weirdest Places*, this collection of sincere, funny, and to-the-point motivational advice instructs, entertains and inspires." **Cherlyn Bradley**, Editor, *The Chemical Bulletin*

"Rob's stories have touched and helped me. Always providing a quick smile with the words of wisdom said so simply, the concepts seemed like common sense. He may the Walt Whitman of our day." **Emory M. Counts**, Director, Florida Community Development Association

"Robert Wilson has the gift of grabbing your attention and taking you along for the ride! A master story-teller, Wilson combines the honesty, wisdom, and sparkling insight of the mentor you always wanted. He is the real deal - the master of motivation! I enjoy Robert's work because of the deft way that the message is woven into the story. People remember stories." **Amy Wainright**, Sunrise Guided Visualizations

"Rob's stories are always spot on; spinning a message from his real-world experiences with quick-witted, powerful endings. His stories keep the members of our organization always yearning for more." **Linda Otto**, Executive Director, International Medical and Dental Hypnotherapy Association

Wisdom in the Weirdest Places

How to Motivate Yourself and Others

*A collection of Inspirational Stories from
The Un-Comfort Zone*

by **Robert Evans Wilson, Jr.**

cover design by Kevin Tester

Copyright © 2013 Robert Evans Wilson, Jr.

All rights reserved. No part of this book may be reproduced or utilized in any form or by any means, electronic or mechanical, including photocopying, recording, or by any information storage and retrieval system, without the prior written permission of the author. Inquiries should be addressed to Robert Wilson at uncomfortzone@gmail.com.

ISBN-10: 061593479X
ISBN-13: 978-0615934792

To my sister Cindy, who has always been there for me

ACKNOWLEDGMENTS

I would like to thank all of the publishers and editors who have run *The Un-Comfort Zone* column in their magazines and newspapers. In particular, I would like to thank Cynthia Bailey, Editor-in-Chief of *Transaction World Magazine*, for being the very first. Thank you also to Lybi Ma, Senior Editor at *Psychology Today* for running it as a blog. And, thank you to Ronnie Jones, Publisher; Bonnie Love, Editor; and Michele Stevens, Office Administrator at *Worldwide Drilling Resources* magazine for running it the longest.

TABLE OF CONTENTS

INTRODUCTION .... **XV**

CHAPTER ONE - CHALLENGES 1
What's Pushing Your Buttons?
  Why drawing a line in the sand moves us 2
I Dare You to Read This
  What challenges you to excel? 4
What Perplexing Puzzle Is Piquing Your Curiosity?
  It doesn't take a great mind to solve mysteries 7
What's Holding You Back?
  If traditional methods aren't working for you, change your
  perception 9

CHAPTER TWO - DESIRE 11
What Drives Your Desire?
  When was the last time you were obsessed with something? 12
The Pleasure Principle
  What is it that you can't wait to do every day? 14
The Reward is in the Eye of the Beholder
  Learn what someone values for the key to motivate them 16
Life Lessons from My Cat
  The problem was I had been following the Golden Rule 18
Not Gonna Hold My Breath
  Hope is "the" last ditch motivator 20
Seeking Danger to Find a Sense of Life
  Thrills unveil your mortality and make you feel alive 22
Law of Attraction for People Who Don't Believe in Voodoo
  If you find wishing on a star difficult to swallow 25
The Perfect Ad
  People are motivated by solutions 27

CHAPTER THREE - FEAR 31
The Most Powerful Motivator
  How fear is etched into our brains 32

Change Please
Motivation means you're either moving toward or away from something *34*
Defeating the De-Motivator
When seeds of doubt creep into consciousness *36*
The Second Mouse Gets the Cheese
It's the willingness to take risks that defines the innovator *38*
Instead Of Serving It Cold... Don't Serve It at All
Revenge is a survival instinct dating back to our caveman days *41*
What's Keeping You Awake?
Worry feels like motivation but it is actually a de-motivator *43*
KA-BOOM! The Explosive Pain of Shame
Shame is so powerful it can make you feel worthless *45*
Deadlines Work
Put yourself in a box in order to think outside of it *48*

CHAPTER FOUR – STATUS AND PRESTIGE 51
Pack Mentality
Humans are as motivated by status as pack animals *52*
You'll Know When You've Arrived
Are status symbols behind you? Probably not! *54*
Good Habit - Questionable Motive
Exposing yourself to new things creates opportunity *56*

CHAPTER FIVE - CONNECTION 59
Craving Connection
We desire relationships because they make us feel important *60*
Lubricate with Laughter
There's integrity in humor because true laughter can't be forced *62*
How Cool are You?
What is it that really makes someone cool? *65*
Facebook Drama Triangle
Storming in on a white horse can cost you a friend *67*
The Victory of Vulnerability
Rolling over can be amazingly powerful *69*
Be True to Yourself
Trying to impress the wrong people has a high price *72*

Love Makes You Do Stupid Things
When you love yourself you attract respect..................................74
Will Fame Buy Me Love?
What is it in your past that motivates you today? 77
Who is the Puppet Master of Your Story?
Is your subconscious mind pulling the strings? 79

CHAPTER SIX – POWER AND LEADERSHIP 83
Leadership vs. Power
Are you driven by goals or by power over others? 84
Keep Your Power
Giving your power to bullies robs you of confidence and motivation..86
Fear vs. Power
There is a correlation between fear and the amount of power people seek 88
We Empower Bullies with Our Admiration
You love bullies... when they are on your side 92
Empathy for Bullies
Finding the motivation that drives bullies to attack....................94
The Buck Starts Here
Looking for motive? Follow the money trail.............................97
On my Honor
Is the concept of honor simply too difficult to understand? 99
Example is Everything
Whether you intend to or not, you lead by example 102

CHAPTER SEVEN – MAKING BOLD COMMITMENTS 105
What's the Worst that can Happen?
Being bold has enormous rewards..106
Take the Plunge
Commit by jumping in feet first, then watch where it takes you 108
The Magic of Commitment is no Mystery
How opportunities arise that you ordinarily would not notice .111
It's Your Pride and Vanity, Stupid
Let yourself be embarrassed - it's worth it!..............................114

CHAPTER EIGHT – BELIEVING IN YOURSELF..117
The Main Ingredient
A recipe for success needs this secret 118
Copy Cats Climb the Ladder of Success Faster
Sometimes observing another doing it is enough.....................120
Attaboy!
Recognition doesn't have to be tangible to be effective 122
Criticism Sucks
Subtle criticism hurts as much as getting ripped a new one 124
More Powerful than You Know
The least bit of praise can be powerfully motivating 126
Chill Out
The trick is to take your mind off the prize..............................128
Don't Hold Back!
If you believe you can - then STOP over-thinking it 130

CHAPTER NINE - ADVERSITY 133
Will You Freak-Out or Hunker Down?
How do you handle a crisis?..134
Thrown into the Driver's Seat
When leadership is needed, will you rise to the occasion? 136
Bouncing off the Bottom
It is human nature to go backwards before going forward.......138
Is Pain a Motivator?
I feel your pain; actually, it's mine, but it helps me understand yours 140
The Crash After the Crush
Intense emotional pain drove me to discover its true source 143
Don't Get Stuck in Reverse
It's hard to hit a target facing the wrong direction 146
STOP Bugging Me!
Things that irritate you are very motivating 150
This Story has a Happy Ending... I Promise!
Adversity motivates you to focus on what is really important...153

CHAPTER TEN – GAINING MOMENTUM 157
The Examined Life
Knowledge gives you the confidence to take a risk...................158

The First Million
    Seductive and intoxicating, success breeds more success.........*160*
Keeping the Ball Rolling
    Momentum is the point when success comes easily *162*

CHAPTER ELEVEN - EMPATHY..........................165
Empathy on Empty
    Fill up your tank with this business boosting tool.....................*166*
Bleed It Out
    *Some advertising is designed to speak to your
    subconscious mind*...*169*
Forget the Facts - Tell a Story
    Using narrative to translate your mission into human terms....*171*

CHAPTER TWELVE - PASSION.............................175
Good Stuff also Comes in Threes
    Love is a foundation for confidence, creativity and growth......*176*
Compelled by an Idea
    Sometimes an idea is so exciting you can't leave it alone.........*178*
Sometimes You Have to Rip the Cover Off
    *Discover someone's passion and you'll know what
    motivates them*..*180*
Mmmm... the Way You Move Me
    Music plucks your emotions like a guitar string *182*

INTRODUCTION

The idea for *Wisdom in the Weirdest Places* was born in 1998 when I was asked, as the author of *OFF THE WALL! The Best Graffiti off the Walls of America*, to give a humorous motivational speech to the Southern Association of Gasoline Retailers. *OFF THE WALL!* is an illustrated collection of bathroom graffiti. It seemed to me that gas station owners would already have their fill of that sort of thing from their own bathrooms, but I was happy to get the gig.

As I sat down to write the speech, I thought about all the funny graffiti I'd collected over the years, and wondered how I might use it to motivate people in achieving their goals. Then it dawned on me that some of it actually offered some pretty decent wisdom.

So, that was how I began the speech, by suggesting to the audience that some of the graffiti I'd collected offered good advice. I received some skeptical looks, which fed right into the humor I was setting up. I said, "You don't believe me. Well, here's a great example, it's the only graffiti I ever found in an airplane bathroom:

If at first you don't succeed, then skydiving is not for you.

That generated a laugh, so I offered the next one which I reported finding at an Optimist Club meeting. "Here's some advice that's better than having a friend who works in a bank:

Borrow money from pessimists - they don't expect it back.

More laughter, and I continued with several more.

Never fry bacon naked.

It's always darkest before dawn. So if you're going to steal your neighbor's newspaper, that's the time to do it.

No man has ever been shot while doing the dishes.

And, then I shifted gears somewhat to graffiti that did offer sound advice:

Letting the cat out of the bag is a whole lot easier than putting it back in.

Knowledge is knowing a tomato is a fruit. Wisdom is not putting it in a fruit salad.

Then one more that set the tone for the serious part of the speech:

The only difference between a rut and a grave is the depth.

"And that last one brings me to the theme of this speech which is Goals Are Important, so important they can even extend your life. I'd like to offer you some methods for achieving your goals by sharing with you some stories about how I have reached my goal of becoming a successful writer."

I began by telling how I knew I wanted to be a writer as early as 3rd grade. I recalled the time I told my dad that I wanted to be a writer when I grew up. How he laughed, then said, "Writing is not a job; writing is a hobby."

That was not what I wanted to hear. I wanted someone who would validate my dream, but it wasn't to come while I was in elementary school. It wasn't until 8th grade that I would get an indication that I might make it as a writer. It would come with an "F" on an English paper. That's right the grade of "F" as in "Failure." I was assigned a book report. I got the book, read it, wrote the report, and turned it in.

A few days later, my English teacher rolled into the classroom with an overhead projector and announced, "Today I'm going to teach you how to write a book report by showing you examples of your classmates' work. You'll see an "A" paper, a "B" paper, a "C" paper, and even an "F" paper. There was a titter about the room as we all wondered who got the "F."

She started with the "A" paper which she projected onto the screen in the front of the classroom. "Suzy Smith gets an "A" because she dotted all her "i"s and crossed all her "t"s." The next paper was the "B" paper. "Joey Jones gets a "B" because he did this, but didn't do that." Next was the "C" paper. "Blah, blah, blah..." Finally, she put the "F" paper on the screen. And, there it was, a big black "F" right beside my name.

Have you ever gotten that sick sinking feeling in your stomach when you're surprised to find out you've done something wrong? It's called Shame, and I was stunned by it. I was actually shocked, because I had never gotten an "F" before. I was always an "A" or a "B" student.

Then she started to explain. "Rob Wilson gets an "F" on his paper because he plagiarized his work. Plagiarism means that he copied his work from the book he was supposed to read. I say 'supposed' to read, because I don't believe he read this book at all. He copied his book report directly from the inside flap of the book's dust jacket."

All of sudden that sick feeling went away and it was replaced with elation. The teacher could see my smiling face through the dimmed lights of the classroom, and walked up to me. She pointed her finger at my face and said, "Robert Wilson, what are smiling about? Plagiarism is a serious offence!"

I replied, "I'm smiling because I didn't copy my book report from the book. I actually wrote it! And, if you think I copied it, then I must write as well as an adult author who is published."

When I said that, she got all flustered and yanked my paper off the overhead projector. She then said, "Well, I'll have to go to the library and look at that book for myself."

True to her word, a few days later, she announced to the class. "I've been to the library, and Rob Wilson did not copy his book report from the book. However, he does not get an "A." She then gloatingly added, "On closer examination, I found two grammatical errors that an adult author who is published would never have made." (She didn't announce it to the class, but she gave me an "A-")

That teacher would not become the one who would inspire me directly. Although my writing was good enough to make her believe I had copied it, she never went on to give me praise or encouragement. I had embarrassed her - albeit inadvertently - in front of the class. In her mind, I was an enemy. Nevertheless, she encouraged indirectly. I was thrilled that she had accused me of plagiarism. If she had not done that, and simply given me an "A," it would never have impacted my writing confidence. For that I'm eternally grateful! And, it's a pretty weird way in which to gain motivation.

That incident sustained my belief that I could be a writer. The following year I got an English teacher who would actually encourage me by praising my writing skills. You will learn about her in Chapter Eight with the article *More Powerful Than You Know*.

I went on to share several more stories on the importance of goals and how to motivate yourself to achieve them. Many of which inspired the articles in this book. Also, in my speech, I still needed to pay off my theme of graffiti that actually provided sound advice. So, I included a story about how one bit of graffiti actually encouraged me to get my writing career back on track after I'd left writing for a job as a traveling salesman.

It was a job I didn't like, but it paid well. After four years of being on the road, and away from family and friends, I grew weary of all the travel. During that time I didn't write any articles or fiction, just some sales related materials for the business. I found the graffiti one night when I stopped for gas, after having been on the road for two weeks straight. While there I visited the men's room. Above the urinal I saw a classic bit of graffiti I'd seen a hundred times before:

We aim to please, you aim too please.

Just below that was written:

We rarely hit where we do not aim.

At the time I thought it was just a variation on a theme, but jotted it down for my collection anyway.

When I got back on the road, that bit of graffiti kept creeping into my thoughts. After a while it dawned on me that it meant so much more than not peeing on the floor. I realized that I was no longer aiming at my goal of becoming a writer. The more I thought about it, the more determined I became to get back to writing. When I finished that trip, I gave my notice, and started writing again. I wrote for newspapers, I wrote advertising, and I started working on my fiction again. Within a short time, I was making money writing and was in the career I wanted. Later on I learned that those words, which had motivated me so much, were actually the words of Henry David Thoreau.

I closed my speech by sharing the story of Jeanne Calment, whose resolve to achieve one goal resulted in her incidentally achieving a world record that no one has yet to beat. You will read about what motivated her in the first chapter of this book with the article *What's Pushing Your Buttons?*

Long before I wrote that speech, I was a student of motivation. I've been curious about human motivation since I was a teenager. I always wanted to know, "What makes people tick?"

Back when I was in high school I started my search for the answer to that question by subscribing to the magazine *Psychology Today*. I also read every pop-psychology book I could get my hands on: *I'm OK, You're OK* by Thomas Harris, *Games People Play* by Eric Berne, *When I Say No, I Feel Guilty* by Manuel Smith, and *How to Win Friends and Influence People* by Dale Carnegie to name a few.

Still full of questions when I started college, I studied psychology and philosophy in order to find the answers I sought. I took a job working in a psychiatric hospital to take my education even further. Those were heady days for me as a 19 year old. I participated in group therapy; handled crisis intervention on the phone; and listened to patients and charted their feelings. I loved all the responsibility.

When I finished college, I applied my knowledge of human motivation in the advertising industry. I developed compelling messages that would move people to the next step of the buying process.

My success in advertising won me several prestigious awards, and invitations to teach at four colleges. I took one of those teaching opportunities which in turn led to my speaking on advertising around the United States. Overtime, the speeches I was giving became more motivational in nature.

Then in February 2007, while I was serving as Cubmaster to my children's Cub Scout pack, I had a conversation about motivation with one of the den mothers. Cynthia Bailey was the editor of Transaction World magazine, and she invited me to write a column on motivation. I titled the column *The Un-Comfort Zone* as a play on words with the popular cliché that says; in order to succeed you must get out of your comfort zone.

Motivation is all about motion or movement. In other words, if you are comfortable, if you are happy and content, then you DO NOT move. You do not change. Why would you? On the other hand, if you are uncomfortable, if you're unhappy, then you want to change. You want to move back toward your comfort zone. There are thousands of motivators, and all of us at any one time are being urged by a dozen or more: Hunger, Safety, Sex, Love, Enlightenment to name just a few.

Interestingly, you can take all those motivators and boil them down to a variation of two basic emotions: Fear and Desire. You are either moving toward something you desire; or you are moving away from something you fear.

Over the next few years, The *Un-Comfort Zone* was picked up by hundreds of magazines and newspapers. Including *Psychology Today* which was where I began my search for answers as a teenager. For this book, I have selected the most popular articles from my column. In the following pages, we will explore the various aspects of motivation, and how you can motivate yourself and others including: employees, customers, friends, loved ones and children. We'll examine further the ways in which motivation works from intrinsic motivation (finding the drive within you) to extrinsic motivation (outside factors that will influence you).

In many ways *Wisdom in the Weirdest Places* represents my journey, how I've learned to find personal ambition, as well as, uncovering the causes that kept me from reaching my dreams. These are the stories that have inspired me or taught me how to inspire others. Some are the stories of friends, family, even famous people that I found helpful, and then there are my personal stories where I occasionally allow myself to be completely vulnerable in discussing the trials I endured to learn these lessons.

I have grouped the articles into chapters by key motivator. However, don't feel that you have to read them in order. Each article was written to stand alone. I hope you enjoy reading them as much as I enjoyed writing them.

Rob Wilson, December 2013

CHAPTER ONE - CHALLENGES

In this first chapter, the weird places I acquire wisdom are from a cantankerous old woman who wants to stick it to a lawyer, an old hatbox, and a bicycle with no pedals.

We'll start by looking at how challenges motivate us. Whether the challenge is an obstacle, a boundary, a person, or a personal belief, it can be overcome.

I begin with the very first article I wrote for my column. It seems fitting since this was the story that motivated me to begin writing on the topic of motivation.

It is the story of Jeanne Marie Calment, who, in overcoming a challenge, broke a world record. It has yet to be beaten. The wisdom in her story is how she proved - perhaps unintentionally - just how valuable having goals can be.

Next we will look at variety of different challenges such as how an employer can motivate an employee. And, how an advertiser can stimulate your curiosity by issuing a challenge.

Then we will look at how a mystery creates a unique sort of challenge that is driven by our sense of curiosity.

Finally we will look at how our personal beliefs can create the most difficult challenges to overcome. We will see how wisdom can be found simply by looking at your challenge in a different way.

Robert Evans Wilson, Jr.

What's Pushing Your Buttons?

Why drawing a line in the sand moves us

    What motivates you? Are you motivated by fame, fortune or fear? Or is it something deeper that fans the flames inside of you. Perhaps you are like Jeanne Louise Calment whose burning desire enabled her to do something that no other human being has done before. A feat so spectacular that it generated headlines around the globe, got her a role in a motion picture, and landed her in the *Guinness Book of World Records*. A record that has yet to be beaten.

    Jeanne Louise, however, did not initially motivate herself. It was someone else who drew the line in the sand. But, it became a line she was determined to cross.

    In motivation we talk about getting outside of one's comfort zone. It is only when we are uncomfortable that we begin to get motivated. Usually to get back into our comfort zone as quickly as possible.

    Born into the family of a middle-class store owner, Calment was firmly entrenched in her comfort zone. At age 21 she married a wealthy store owner and lived a life of leisure. She pursued her hobbies of tennis, the opera, and sampling France's famous wines. Over the years she met Impressionist painter Van Gogh; watched the erection of the Eiffel Tower; and attended the funeral of *Hunchback of Notre Dame* author, Victor Hugo.

    Twenty years after her husband passed away, she had reached a stage in life where she had pretty much achieved everything that she was going to achieve. Then along came a lawyer. The lawyer made Jeanne Louise a proposition. She accepted it. He thought he was simply making a smart business deal. Inadvertently he gave her a goal. It took her 30 years to achieve it, but achieve it she did.

    Are you willing to keep your goals alive for 30 years? At what point do you give up? Thomas Edison never gave up, instead he said, "I have not failed. I've just found 10,000 ways that won't work." Winston Churchill during the bleakest hours of World War II kept an entire country motivated with this die-hard conviction: "We shall defend our Island, whatever the cost may be, we shall fight on the beaches... in the fields and in the streets... we shall never surrender."

Wisdom in the Weirdest Places

Many of us give up too soon because we set limits on our goals. Achieving a goal begins with determination. Then it's just a matter of our giving them attention and energy.

When Jeanne Louise was 92 years old, attorney François Raffray, age 47, offered to pay her $500 per month (a fortune in 1967) for the rest of her life, if she would leave her house to him in her will. According to the actuarial tables it was a great deal. Here was an heirless woman who had survived her husband, children, and grandchildren. A woman, who was just biding her time, with nothing to live for. That is until Raffray came along and offered up the *sucker bet* that she would soon die. It was motivation enough for Jeanne, who was determined to beat the lawyer. Thirty years later, Raffray became the "sucker" when he passed away first at age 77.

When asked about this by the press, Calment simply said, "In life, one sometimes makes bad deals." Having met her goal, Jeanne passed away five months later. But on her way to this end, she achieved something else: at 122 years old, she became the oldest person to have ever lived.

Goals will keep you alive. I recall having seen several studies of people who live 100 years or more. Not surprisingly, these studies indicated that having goals is one of the top traits of centenarians.

Don't wait until someone draws a line in the sand for you. Challenge yourself to live your dreams. Put your goals in writing, and then formulate a plan for reaching them. If it takes a hundred years to achieve them, enjoy the journey - that's what it is all about anyway.

Question for discussion or continued thought:

What has challenged you lately? Was it a person, a problem, an obstacle, an idea, or a task?

Robert Evans Wilson, Jr.

I Dare You to Read This

What challenges you to excel?

A reader of my column wrote me to suggest that rather than trying to encourage someone, a better way to motivate them is to issue a challenge. So, I felt challenged to write about it.

Whenever I think of laying down a challenge, I think of a classic story about Charles Schwab the magnate of Bethlehem Steel. One day, he was visiting his least productive mill to discover why it was underperforming. During his inspection, he discovered that everything seemed to be in order: the workers all knew their jobs, the equipment was top-notch, and the manager highly educated. Despite all of that, it was producing far behind all his others.

He ended his tour of the facility a few minutes before shift change. Stopping in front of one the furnaces, he asked a worker, "How many heats has your shift made today?" "Six," the man replied. Schwab then asked for a piece of chalk. He took it, wrote a large number "6" on the floor, and then left the building.

When the second shift arrived, they saw the chalked "6" on the floor, and inquired about it. "The big boss was in here today," said one of the men. "He asked us how many heats we made, and we told him six. He chalked it down."

The next morning Schwab visited the same mill. He saw that the "6" had been erased by the second shift and a large number "7" written in its place. He returned to the mill again at the end of first shift, where he saw that the "7" had been replaced with a "10." With a piece of chalk, Schwab started a lively competition that continued until that mill was producing more than any other.

This particular challenge worked because it pitted the esprit de corps of two teams against each other. I'm not sure that particular challenge would work today with the added burden of government regulations and union rules.

I also believe that a challenge does not stand alone as a motivator. There has to be something behind it. It may be pride, prestige, or fear that drives the need to overcome the obstacle.

Challenges are always obstacles whether it is an athletic, academic, intellectual, work-related, health-related, a personal goal

Wisdom in the Weirdest Places

or a personal tragedy. Sometimes the challenge is given by a boss, a team mate, a spouse, or simply the zeitgeist.

Many times a challenge will be issued with the following words: "I'll bet you can't..." or "I dare you to..."

A challenger draws a line in the sand and defies us to cross it. Hmmm, isn't that what the game of American football is all about?

Back when I was graduating from high school, I had been nominated for the *Atlanta Journal* Cup which was sponsored by the newspaper of the same name. It was touted as the highest award given to a member of the senior class. What it was actually given for was left up to the school, but more often than not, it was a leadership award. I was nominated for being President of the Student Council; my rival was nominated because he was Senior Class President. He won. I received what my classmates considered to be the second place award: a copy of William Danforth's book: *I Dare You!*

I was so disappointed that I didn't crack the book for months, but when I finally did I was quite surprised. The *"I Dare You" Award* specifically states that it is given for leadership. And, each chapter dares you to seek excellence in a number of life's pursuits. I found the book to be quite motivating, and have read it many times over the years. I've even read it to my children. I'm finding that my second place award has lasting value that continues to give year after year.

The advertising industry loves to use a challenge to get us to try their product or service. We frequently see words such as "Take the Taste Test," or "Give Us 30 Days and You'll Become a Believer." I remember this one from *Gillette*: "Take the SensorExcel Challenge: One shave and we bet you'll get rid of your disposable razor for good." Perhaps the most famous challenge ad is this one: "Be All That You Can Be: In The Army."

We love fun challenges such as problems that stimulate our ingenuity: crossword puzzles and Sudoku for example. We enjoy the challenge of improving our skill at games and sports. OK, the love/hate challenge of golf notwithstanding.

Ultimately, all our challenges are self-given because it is human nature to want to improve. Pablo Picasso said it best, "I am always doing that which I cannot do, in order that I may learn how to do it."

The personal challenges we give ourselves create the journey known as life. Enjoy the pitfalls and peaks as they come because as

Leo Buscaglia, author and professor, put it most bluntly, "Death is a challenge. It tells us not to waste time."

I challenge you to heed his advice and get on with the important things in your life.

Question for discussion or continued thought:

Who has dared you to more than you thought you could be? Did you rise to the challenge?

Wisdom in the Weirdest Places

What Perplexing Puzzle Is Piquing Your Curiosity?

It doesn't take a great mind to solve mysteries

The next hatbox I pulled off the top shelf of the closet nearly tipped me off the ladder. It was the weight that surprised me; it was far too heavy for just a hat. As I regained my balance, I wondered why this one weighed more than the others. I set it on the vanity and started untying the strings.

I was curious if it would reveal any secrets about my mother, although I wasn't expecting too much. All the other hatboxes contained... well, actual hats. Women's hats from the 1950s and 60s with velvet, lace, feathers, and fur. It was a bittersweet nostalgia trip as my family inventoried the contents of my mother's house. She had passed away six months earlier.

I lifted the lid and found photographs. Hundreds of black and white photos... some of them dating back to the American Civil War. They were photos I had never seen before. Pictures of people... presumably relatives... but I didn't know that for sure. It was a mystery, and one that I knew I would have to solve.

Looking at those photos one at a time was overwhelming, so one day I took them into my living room. I pushed all the furniture back to the walls, and then spread the photos out on the floor. For the next several days I played the match game. Matching faces and places. Luckily, a few of them had inscriptions on the back that revealed names, dates and locations.

Once I had categorized the photos into groups, I met with my one living relative who was old enough to possibly know who some of these people were. The information she gave me added an entire branch to my family tree. I then started searching the internet where the floodgates opened.

Over the next few years, I found myself on a genealogical journey that did more than just place names to faces. It led me to recognize that my family's dysfunction didn't begin with my parents, but had a pattern that had been passed down generation after generation. And, that gave me the insight I needed to work on it (see Chapter Five: *Who is the Puppet Master of Your Story?*).

A good mystery is compelling and we are motivated to find the answer. A mystery, however, is just a problem that needs to be solved. And, some of them really need to be solved.

I love the story of how Edward Jenner, a country doctor in England, created the smallpox vaccine. In 1762, when he was 13, Edward overheard a milkmaid say, "I shall never have smallpox for I have had cowpox. I shall never have an ugly pockmarked face." It was a statement that would stay in the back of his mind for decades. He had heard all his life that milkmaids were in some mysterious way protected from smallpox. Perhaps this woman had the answer that would save the millions of people who died of smallpox every year. Thirty-three years later, he would find out.

In 1796, he drained fluid from the cowpox lesions on a milkmaid's hands, and then injected it into an eight year old boy. The boy only suffered a mild fever. Two months later, he injected the boy with smallpox. The boy did not get sick - he was protected. Jenner named his new procedure vaccination. 183 years later, smallpox was eradicated from the planet.

It doesn't take a great mind to solve mysteries; just a curious one. Average people do it all the time. There is probably a mystery you can solve that will improve your business. If you think about it, every product and service you purchase began as a solution to a problem. Whether it is through necessity or simple desire, people find new ways of doing things through creative thinking that was stimulated by a mystery. What mystery do you want to solve?

Question for discussion or continued thought:

What puzzle or mystery has piqued your curiosity and driven you to learn more?

Wisdom in the Weirdest Places

What's Holding You Back?

*If traditional methods aren't working for you,
change your perception*

I noticed the training wheels on my son's bike were no longer touching the ground. He was riding without them. "Let's take those off," I said.

"No Daddy, I'm not ready."

"Sure you are; let's give it a try."

After I removed them, he got on the bike, but couldn't get enough momentum to stay up and fell right over.

"See Daddy, I can't do it. Put them back on."

"Let's try it again, this time I'll push." I grabbed the back of the seat and started pushing him. He was pedaling and riding perfectly, and I had to run as fast as I could to continue holding the seat. "You're doing it!" I cried. "I'm going to let go now."

"No Daddy, don't let go. I can't do it."

I let go, and he stopped pedaling. The bike rolled a few more feet, began to wobble, then fell over.

"I can't do it. Daddy, please put the training wheels back on."

He couldn't see what I saw: that he was already riding without them. He was like a circus elephant tied to a stake in the ground. That elephant is strong enough to push over a tree, yet because she was tied to a stake as a baby - when she wasn't strong enough to pull it up - she continues to believe it can't be done.

Greek Stoic philosopher, Epictetus, observed in the first century: "Men are disturbed not by things, but by the view which they take of them." I'd like to rephrase that, "We are held back by our perception of things."

When we encounter challenges in life, we attempt to resolve them with what we know to be true. When that doesn't work we're stumped. Today in business we're stumped by recession, international competition, high taxes and government regulation. We're boxed in. We need to follow the advice of Albert Gyorgyi, the Nobel Prize winning scientist, who discovered vitamin C, "Discovery consists of seeing what everybody has seen and thinking what nobody has thought."

Easier said than done. The trick to "thinking what nobody has thought," begins with changing our perception. Again, easier said than done. The trick to changing your perception can be accomplished by changing your perspective... changing the view which you take of things.

In the classic motion picture, *Dead Poets Society*, an English teacher has his students stand on their desks to change their perspective. He says, "We must constantly look at things in different ways."

You can read a dozen books on how to think creatively, and each of the techniques you learn will be to accomplish just one thing: changing the way you look at the problem. By looking at it from a different perspective, you will begin to see different solutions.

With my son, I continued to push the bike and run as fast as I could. After falling down a few more times, he finally got it, and was able to ride on his own. I would have given anything to spare him the pain and the tears.

Someone else, much more creative than me, saw the problem from a different perspective and came up with a better solution. It is called the "balance bike." Seeing that children became dependent on training wheels, this unknown person asked the question, "What if, I didn't have training wheels?"

The solution was to take the pedals off, and let children learn to balance on the bike first by walking it along. As the children's skills improve, they will lengthen their strides until they can lift their feet off the ground and coast. Once this is accomplished, the pedals can be put back on the bike, and the problem of becoming dependent on training wheels is eliminated.

It is human nature to constantly improve the way we do things. If the traditional way of doing things isn't working for you, then change your perception. Ask yourself what you would do if the current solution did not exist. Now you're looking at it from a different perspective. You'll be amazed with what you will come up with!

Question for discussion or continued thought:

What problem are you facing that viewing it from a new perspective would help?

CHAPTER TWO - DESIRE

In this chapter, I gain wisdom from horror movies, buying lottery tickets, and having my hair cut against my will.

We'll look at how desire is the most common motivator because there are so many things we want that we believe will make our lives better: a new job, car, house, clothing, and the list goes on.

The problem may be that desire is not always a potent enough motivator to help us reach our goals. When we cannot achieve our goals, that desire can become the foundation for envy, which is one of the most destructive emotions.

In the first article, we will look at when desire does become powerful enough to help us reach our goal. I do this by sharing a story of a time when I was completely obsessed with owning a very specific item. Nothing else would do - I had to have it! Throughout the rest of this chapter we will look at other aspects of desire that move us.

We will examine how to use desire to motivate others such as family members, employees, and customers. And, we'll look at Hope, Law of Attraction, and how I obtained the wisdom to stop using the Golden Rule from my cat.

Robert Evans Wilson, Jr.

What Drives Your Desire?

When was the last time you were obsessed with something?

It was love at first sight. I was a 15 year old working as a parking lot cashier, when a brand new car pulled up to the booth. I'd never seen anything like it; it was a new model from *Toyota* called *Celica*. Approaching the legal driving age, I dreamed of owning a car. Now my dream had a form. For the next two years, I saved all my money and during that time a Celica couldn't come within my peripheral vision without my noticing it. It was the only car I wanted. I went to the showroom dozens of times to sit in it, feel it, smell it. I talked with every owner of one who passed through my parking lot. I was driven.

Unfortunately, a new one was too expensive, so I looked in the newspaper every day for a used one, but I was always more than $1,000 short. At 17 and half years old, borrowing my parent's car was painful. The desire and the peer pressure to own a car – any car – was nearly overwhelming, and my dream was wavering. My friends began suggesting cars that I could afford. Then my Dad introduced me to a car wholesaler. When I met with him, I reluctantly gave him a list of cars I thought I could afford. As we talked about them, he seemed to sense my lack of enthusiasm. He pressed me, "Are there any others you're interested in?" "Well... there's the Toyota Celica," I replied, "but I know I can't afford it." He jotted it down and said, "You let me worry about that." My eyes lit up as he asked me about colors and options. Then he drew a big circle around the word Celica. Less than a week later, he phoned me. He found one I could afford. It had a small dent in the fender which I could fix for under $100. Cha-ching, desire satisfied.

When was the last time you were obsessed with something? Desire is a powerful motivator, but unlike Fear it cannot be easily triggered. Oh, sure, I can create a television ad depicting a thick juicy steak sizzling on a grill and make your mouth water. Maybe I can even get you off the couch and into your car to go get one. As a marketer, an employer, or even as a parent, I can plant the seeds of desire, but in order for it to blossom, it must develop from within. Once it takes root, desire has the amazing ability to drive itself. When it becomes very powerful, we call it ambition. So few people reach this level of want, that we use the word "Hunger" to describe it... because hunger is a desire that everyone can understand.

When you observe the world's most successful people - - in business, sports, or politics - - you see that Desire takes precedence over every other aspect of their lives. As Frank Sinatra sings in *I've Got You Under My Skin*: "I'd sacrifice anything come what might." Most of us have many things we are unwilling to sacrifice. Family and friends are two of the most common. Winners give their Desire complete attention, focus and energy. Michael Jordan is an excellent example; he became one of the greatest basketball players by making 2000 practice shots every day. Are you that dedicated to your dream?

On the other hand, perhaps you gain more satisfaction from your hobbies than your work. In that case, you probably wish you could spend more time pursuing them instead of your job. That is because pleasure is the force that fans the flames of Desire. Marsha Sinetar in her book *Do What You Love the Money Will Follow* writes: "When you study people who are successful...it is abundantly clear that their achievements are directly related to the enjoyment they derive from their work." Are you ready to give up everything for your Desire?

Question for discussion or continued thought:

Is there an aspect of your favorite hobby that you could apply to your work?

Robert Evans Wilson, Jr.

The Pleasure Principle

What is it that you can't wait to do every day?

Swing and miss. "Strike Two." cried the umpire. I threw one more pitch right in at the player's wrists. He swung hard, but the ball just dribbled right back to the pitcher's mound. I picked it up and gently tossed it to the first baseman for the out.

As the batter turned back toward the dugout, his team captain stepped out and screamed, "Darrell, you've got to get over your fear of this guy!"

The words poured like sweet honey into my ears.

It was the third time I had gotten him out that night including two strike outs. I had completely shut down the best hitter on the best team in the league. It was the most fun I'd had in weeks.

No, I wasn't throwing heat. Quite the contrary, I'm talking about slow-pitch recreational softball for the over-thirty crowd.

But, I was totally into it. Once a week I stood on the mound under the lights with everyone's eye on me. Despite the butterflies in my stomach, I can't image anything more exciting (OK, maybe skydiving!).

And, I was totally motivated! I spent several hours each week tossing balls in my driveway. I set up an area with a pitcher's rubber and home plate laid out to the exact dimensions of those on the playing field. After I mastered the two standard softball pitches, I developed two of my own. The best was a softball version of the knuckleball. A spin-less ball that baffled batters the first time they saw it, but even when they did hit it - they could never get any distance on it.

I have friends who are obsessed with golf; others with tennis. None of them have a clue what drives me to play softball. But, then again, I don't get why they play golf or tennis.

What motivates me to play softball or for that matter my friends to play golf and tennis? That's easy... it's fun! It is all about having fun... pleasure is very motivating. We all seek some pleasure in life. It's what keeps us going. And, for those pursuits that we enjoy, we are never too tired; we always seem to find time and energy for them. It comes to us easily. If only we could find that kind of relaxed energy for work.

Wisdom in the Weirdest Places

What is it that you can't wait to do every day? Is it a hobby? A sport? Sigmund Freud described that driving creative spirit as the *Pleasure Principle*. But, he also spoke of a contrasting principle that existed to put the brakes on our desire called the *Death Instinct*. Thankfully that theory has been disproved; however, it's still very true that "all work and no play make Jack a dull boy." Not only dull. Where happiness is absent - health is often absent too.

I look forward to work every day. I have clearly followed the advice of my father who encouraged me to find a job I enjoyed so that I would never "work" a day in my life. But, what should you do if you're not happy in your work? Make changes! That may be easier said than done. So, if you can't change your job, then change your work environment.

It's a well known fact that employees who enjoy their work are more productive. This is so true that people frequently turn down better paying jobs to stay with one that is fun. There are many ways to make your workplace more fun. Authors Dave Hemsath and Leslie Yerkes in their book offer us *301 Ways to Have Fun at Work*. Every company is different so it will be up to you to discover what you can do to make your place of business more fun. But, if you want to motivate your staff – I always say, "Give them something to laugh about!"

Question for discussion or continued thought:

What are some things you can do to make your workplace more fun?

Robert Evans Wilson, Jr.

The Reward is in the Eye of the Beholder

*Learn what someone values for
the key to motivate them*

In the early 1970s I was a young teenager who was completely caught up in the Zeitgeist. I admired the long-haired rebels and radicals who were engaged in protesting the establishment and developing the counter-culture. I didn't really know what any of that meant, but to me it was all about empowering youth and declaring our independence from the adults. My parents in particular.

As with any normal teenager, I was trying to grow up as fast as I could. And, because it annoyed my parents, wearing my hair long was its perfect expression. That and it was de rigueur among all the teenagers who wanted to be cool. So, the longer the better – or in the immortal words from the title song to the 1968 Broadway Musical *HAIR*, "Oh, say can you see, My eyes if you can... Then my hair's too short!"

It drove my parents completely crazy. They could not understand why any male would want to wear long hair. We fought about it all the time.

Meanwhile, I was in my first year of high school and the transition to a new school was causing my grades to drop dramatically. My parents saw an advantage, and the law was laid down: keep my grades above a certain minimum or cut my hair. It worked. I brought home a dismal report card, and it was off to the barber shop. Not surprisingly, my next report card met the minimum.

The formula is simple: if you can find out what is valuable to someone, then you have the key to motivating them. For me, at age 13, the length of my hair became the coin of the realm.

A year later, I accidentally made the Honor Roll. I say it was an accident because I was only trying to meet the minimum grades required by my parents and I somehow exceeded that. When I received the engraved certificate with the embossed gold seal, I was surprised by the feeling it gave me. I felt important – especially when my teachers praised me. I liked that feeling, and I wanted to experience it again. Suddenly the coin of the realm changed, and it was no longer the length of my hair that was motivating me. It was high grades and the sense of pride they gave me. Oh, my hair continued to grow, but my grades were all about achievement. From that point forward until I graduated, I never failed to make the Honor Roll.

Find out what is valuable to the person you want to motivate. What hobbies do they have? What are they passionate about? How do they spend their spare time? Then when you learn what rocks their world, find a way to tie your goals to it.

If you're not sure what is valuable to someone, you can always make them feel important with an award or some other public acknowledgment. Everyone likes to hear their name announced in recognition at company or association meetings. Everyone likes to read their name in print in the organizational newsletter or website. Many business newspapers have a section where you can post your employees promotions and accomplishments. These low-cost to no-cost incentives truly have the power to motivate.

Question for discussion or continued thought:

What do you value the most? How might you use that to motivate yourself?

Robert Evans Wilson, Jr.

Life Lessons from My Cat

*The problem was I had been
following the Golden Rule*

Once upon a time, I met a beautiful, charming and witty woman and fell deeply in love. Over the months we dated I was the consummate romantic. I brought her flowers; wrote heartfelt love letters; and on occasion even sang to her. At one point she remarked that no one had ever treated her better. Then suddenly and unexpectedly she left me. I was devastated. When I asked her why, she replied, "You never listened to me."

I had no clue what she was talking about.

Of course I listened to her. Didn't I know her favorite foods, music and vacation spots? Absolutely! I also knew of her past struggles, her frustrations at work, and even her dreams for the future. Apparently it was not enough. In retrospect, I finally figured out the problem was that I had been too busy following the Golden Rule: "Do unto others as you would have them do unto you."

Remarkably it wasn't my ex-girlfriend who taught me this lesson, it was my cat. One morning while I was enjoying my coffee on the back porch, Roxy came up to my chair and meowed for attention. I picked her up, held her and started rubbing her soft fur. I knew from past experience that she didn't like that, and she immediately began to squirm and try to jump out of my arms. Nevertheless - in the spirit of Albert Einstein's observation that insanity is doing the same thing over and over again and expecting different results - I hoped that she would start liking it.

Finally, I turned her loose on my lap and petted her. She became very affectionate and gave me lots of nudges with her head and purred loudly. I used to think that my other cat, Spike, was the more loving cat because he likes to be held and cuddled, which is of course, what "I" want to do with a cat. Roxy does not like to be cuddled, and when I attempt it all she does is try to escape. I've learned that she still wants loving and wants to give it back, but it has to be her way. I realized it is that behavior which causes many people to see cats as aloof and unresponsive.

As Roxy worked her way around my lap, rubbing her face against my arms, legs, chest and face, I thought, "Everyone comes into our lives for a reason - usually to teach us something." I looked at Roxy and said, "What are you here to teach me?"

Then it dawned on me that she was there to teach me the Platinum Rule: "Do unto others as *they* would have you do unto *them*." In contrast to the Golden Rule which is all about "Me," the Platinum Rule is all about "You." The Golden Rule is about "Controlling." The Platinum Rule is about "Giving."

In other words, to motivate someone, give them what they want. I should have known this intuitively from the years I spent in the advertising business. I have taught hundreds of seminars where I advised my students, "When you create an ad, always put the prospect first; because when they see or hear it, all they are thinking is: What's In It For Me!"

I'm reminded again of the wisdom of Dale Carnegie who noted, "You can make more friends in two months by becoming interested in other people than you can in two years by trying to get other people interested in you." To do that he advises: "Be a good listener; encourage others to talk about themselves; talk in terms of the other person's interests; make them feel important - and do it sincerely."

He then adds, "When dealing with people, let us remember we are not dealing with creatures of logic. We are dealing with creatures of emotion, creatures bustling with prejudices and motivated by pride and vanity."

Now wait a minute... surely, he's talking about cats!

Question for discussion or continued thought:

How can you apply the Platinum Rule to the people in your life?

Robert Evans Wilson, Jr.

Not Gonna Hold My Breath

Hope is "the" last ditch motivator

I bought a lottery ticket. I hope to win. That would be so cool, wouldn't it?

Do I think I'll win? No. I fully understand the odds are against me. Then why did I buy one? I bought it because I've been thinking about *hope* and whether or not it is a powerful motivator.

I recall my friend Brian, who also understands the odds, justifying his weekly purchase of a lottery ticket with this statement, "God can't let you win unless you buy at least one." Brian was full of hope.

Buying a lottery ticket perfectly illustrates our feeling of hope. Once you've bought one, and before the drawing of the winning numbers, you can dream of all the things you'll buy, and all the ways your life will be improved by several million dollars. It's fun to dream; and hope makes us feel better. But, does it improve our lives?

Some of the wisest people who have lived do not think so. Benjamin Franklin said, "He that lives upon hope will die fasting." Friedrich Nietzsche laments, "Hope in reality is the worst of all evils because it prolongs the torments of man." And, Aristotle observed, "Youth is easily deceived because it is quick to hope."

Hope is defined as: "To wish for something with expectation of its fulfillment."

I'm going to vote in the Presidential election. I hope my candidate will win. In the nine times that I previously voted for President, I only voted for the winner once. And then, only because I switched at the last minute to become a single issue voter instead of voting with my core beliefs. I've regretted it ever since.

Since I can't seem to pick a winner, why do I keep voting? Hope of course. Hope for what, you ask? Mostly that the economy will improve, and an environment that is good for business will be fostered. Napoleon Bonaparte probably explained best why I vote, "A leader is a dealer in hope." And, I hope the new guy will fix all the messes I perceive in the country.

I hope for peace and prosperity in the world. There is a certain beauty in hope, it paints a picture of perfection in our minds, and that makes it all the more appealing.

Wisdom in the Weirdest Places

I hope my friend who has cancer will survive. I hope he has hope too because I believe what Russian author, Fyodor Dostoevsky said, "To live without hope is to cease to live."

Hope, however, is an extrinsic motivator. It is what we have when we feel like we have no power to alter the outcome. It is what we have when we depend on external factors to help us. We have given up on making a change by ourselves; we are now dependent on some benevolent force to make our condition better or our dreams come true.

Hope is *the* last ditch motivator. There is a reason why it was on the bottom of Pandora's Box. When we have nothing else left to go on: the concentration camp prisoner, the innocent person on death row, the homeless person who has lost everything; when we are rendered impotent by circumstances; hope motivates us to keep going. That means, as a motivator, hope does have power, or as Roman Senator, Marcus Tullius Cicero noted, "While there's life, there's hope."

Unfortunately, hope is not the type of motivator that is going to help us succeed in life. Success comes from the intrinsic motivation of desire and ambition (and sometimes fear); Napoleon Hill said it best, "Desire is the starting point of all achievement, not a hope, not a wish, but a keen pulsating desire which transcends everything."

While hope makes us feel better, it is not enough; it needs to be backed by commitment and above all action.

Nevertheless, I still hope to win the lottery.

Question for discussion or continued thought:

Is there something you are hoping for? Can you, instead, apply a plan of action to make it happen?

Robert Evans Wilson, Jr.

Seeking Danger to Find a Sense of Life

Thrills unveil your mortality and make you feel alive

After 20 minutes of holding the barrel of a pistol in his mouth, Tom removed it and tossed it onto his bed. He thought of a better way to take himself out - sitting in his garage was a 600cc *Kawasaki Ninja ZX6* motorcycle. He'd always wondered how fast it would go; tonight he was going to find out. Tom was a highly skilled rider who had ridden motorcycles since he was a kid. Now he was going to put those skills to the ultimate test.

He sped onto the highway doing a 60 mph wheelie. It was amazingly invigorating, because for weeks he had been unable to do anything. He was so depressed; he could barely make himself eat. His wife of 10 years had left him, and he felt there was nothing left to live for. He dropped back down onto two wheels and pulled the throttle all the way back. Within seconds he was ripping down the road at 170 mph. He could feel wind screaming in his helmet and mosquitoes smashing into his teeth. Secretly, he hoped the police would spot him and engage him in a chase, for he had no intentions of stopping short of a fiery crash. Fortunately for Tom, at 3A.M. all the cops were busy in doughnut shops, he sped by with impunity.

He took curves so fast his shoulder was only inches from the ground. At one point, he felt his tire slipping in some loose gravel, so he gunned the accelerator harder forcing his tires to grip the pavement below. He drove for hours, always at maximum speed. He was enjoying the adrenaline rush, and it was the happiest he'd felt in weeks. When he realized that he'd survived his death-defying ride, he came to the conclusion that God had other plans for him. Ready to live again, he tapered down to the speed limit and drove home.

Today Tom is happily married. Now he has an easy riding *Harley Davidson* with a windshield, saddlebags, and arm-chair seat in back for his new wife.

Most of us don't need a life-threatening experience to give us a reason to live... however, there is nothing like a good thrill to rejuvenate our spirits!

I have one friend who has been into extreme sports his entire life. Years ago he set up a one-day adventure where he parachuted to a mountain top, skied to the bottom, then got into a kayak for a trip

Wisdom in the Weirdest Places

down a river of white water rapids. Today he gets all he needs by competing in triathlons.

Another friend with more than 4000 jumps from an airplane explained it to me this way, "It's all about the free fall which lasts about 60 seconds, then it's a boring parachute ride to the ground where I pack up my chute and get ready to go again."

Most of us love the pounding heartbeat, rapid breathing, nervous perspiration, and the butterflies in the stomach that come from participating in a hazardous experience. It's that element of fear that stands between a thrill and just plain fun.

For me it's mountain biking. Riding up the mountain is just hard work; the payoff is coming back down. Flying over trails that twist and turn, dip and bump, where I occasionally become airborne. All of that, and the knowledge that if I go too fast or get too close to the edge... I could die.

We enjoy feeling scared. Thrills give us a sense of our mortality and that makes us feel alive. These lyrics from the Sixx:A.M. song *Life Is Beautiful* really grasps that concept:

"*I know some things that you don't*
I've done things that you won't
There's nothing like a trail of blood
to find your way back home
I was waiting for my hearse
What came next was so much worse
It took a funeral to make me feel alive"

Adrenaline junkies keep moving up the ladder of excitement: zip lining, spelunking, bungee jumping, ballooning, scuba diving, mountain climbing, hang gliding, and the scariest one of all: public speaking (OK, I couldn't resist throwing this one in - since it is clearly one of my favorites).

It's all about reaching that feeling we express as, "What a rush!" It feels empowering, and makes us feel that we can do anything. Unfortunately, the feeling is fleeting, but for the few moments it lingers we feel as if we're walking on air.

Unfortunately, some people take their thrill seeking to inappropriate levels, by experimenting with illegal drugs, having sex with strangers, and committing violent crimes like bank robbery. The hangover from any one of those is hardly worth the kick.

Of course there are many safe ways we can get our "Thrill" on: roller coasters, water slides, even horror movies. What exhilarates you? And, how often do you need to get your fix?

Question for discussion or continued thought:

What is your favorite way to get a thrill? Is there a way you can combine it with your work to make it more interesting?

Wisdom in the Weirdest Places

Law of Attraction for People Who Don't Believe in Voodoo

If you find wishing on a star difficult to swallow

The latest fad in motivation is the Law of Attraction or more popularly *The Secret* after the motion picture and book by Rhonda Byrne. The idea being that if you use the power of The Secret you will attract health, wealth and friends to you in abundance.

The Secret takes an old idea and repackages it for today's society. The core idea is that your thoughts control the world around you. If you have positive thoughts, good things come your way. If you have negative thoughts then bad things come your way. In other words, if you wish hard enough for the things you want -- you will get them. Simple. Or is it? If it were simple, then countless people throughout history would have figured it out over and over, and it would not be much of a secret. Perhaps it takes a little more effort than suggested – or perhaps it is just a pipe dream.

We, as modern educated people, need more proof. In order to make it palatable to the skeptic in us, *The Secret* adds an element of science. We are told that quantum physics has identified that all things at the sub-atomic level exist as both particles and as waves – constantly shifting between being solid matter and being pure energy. It is then proposed that our thoughts create brain waves which in turn influence the sub-atomic waves of the entire universe. The Secret claims that the more intent you are in your wish the faster the universe will act upon it. Is it real, or is it Voodoo science?

If real, it sounds wonderful! Now, if I understand correctly, if I wish real hard I can become a concert pianist and play to a sold out audience in Carnegie Hall? I only see one hitch: I've never had a piano lesson in my life.

The Secret also presents the Law of Attraction as if it had been intentionally kept hidden for centuries. That it was suppressed and held by a few conspirators so that they could control all the wealth of the world. Unfortunately, that notion is nothing other than a marketing ploy to generate interest in the book. It also contradicts the concept of Law of Attraction. The idea that a select group of people have kept it away from the masses intentionally preys on the destructively negative emotion of envy.

To the contrary, people who have understood the Law of Attraction have made numerous attempts at sharing it with the world at large. The best example is Andrew Carnegie, who was one of the most successful so-called "Robber Barons" of the Industrial Age. Carnegie hired Napoleon Hill to research the most successful people in the world, how they got that way, and then record his findings in a book. The book is *Think and Grow Rich* and was published in 1937.

The best thing about *Think and Grow Rich* is that it takes the mysticism out of the Law of Attraction. So, for those of you who find wishing on a star a bit difficult to swallow as a method for acquiring wealth, here is the real secret:

Identify your goal. Make a written plan to acquire that goal. Work your plan persistently. Give it your time, attention and energy. The more time and effort you give, the quicker you will achieve it. Visualize it coming to fruition. Draw it, illustrate it, photograph it, then keep it in front of you. Revise your plan as your knowledge grows. Be open-minded to opportunities that arise that may deviate from your plan, but still move you toward your goal.

The world's most successful people were extremely focused on achieving one goal. They focused to the exclusion of everything else including family, friends, lovers, recreation, entertainment, vacations and hobbies.

Next, tell everyone you know about your goal. Spread the word, so that people who can assist you are aware of your intentions. I truly believe that positive minded people attract more opportunities to themselves because they are so pleasant to deal with.

The formula is simple, but most of us compromise our goals because we want to enjoy a full balanced life. A life filled with friends, family and good times. We focus on our goals when time allows, and in turn, our goals take much longer to achieve. The true secret is staying focused on your goal.

Question for discussion or continued thought:

What goal can you give more of your time, attention and energy?

Wisdom in the Weirdest Places

The Perfect Ad

People are motivated by solutions

I saw it on I-75 South heading into Atlanta, Georgia. It was exciting to see -- like spotting the nearly extinct ivory-billed woodpecker. But this was no rare bird; it was a perfect ad. Perhaps just as rare. Five words in black print against a pale purple ground. No design. No graphic device at all. No need; the words said it all. Two of those words were even from the top-ten list of words that generate the strongest response.

The ad presented a clear benefit. It made a powerful offer. It was aimed at a specific target audience. All that in five simple words. The ad was on a billboard, but its message would work in any media: TV, newspaper, radio, magazine, internet, direct mail, or... restroom stall.

It called out only to people who could benefit from the company's products and services. It did not need to entertain anyone. It was not trying to win any awards. It did not waste the time of anyone to whom the message did not pertain. I have no doubt that it has been extremely successful.

Here it is:

20/20 or FREE
Lasik Guarantee

www.woodhams.com
800-639-8474

It's beautiful isn't it? I'd say pure poetry, but you'd think that I was referring to the fact that it happens to rhyme -- that's just a bonus -- it doesn't need to rhyme. Those five words communicate volumes. To a person who is undecided about having eye surgery it says, "Relax, we are so skilled at Lasik -- you will have perfect vision when we're done." An effective sales pitch must dispel the consumer's doubt and instill confidence in its place. This ad does both. By the way, I did not write this ad. Congratulations to the person who did!

But, you're thinking: "Sure, that ad is fine for a specific service like corrective eye surgery, but my company offers a common product with lots of competition that nearly everybody uses. I can't use straight-forward advertising like that. I need to be funny or clever to get attention. Or, I have to speak to the emotions of my customer and get them to relate to my product on a subconscious or visceral level."

Nonsense! That's the image-advertising trap. And, unless you've got millions of ad dollars to spend, I'd stick to the scientifically proven formula of benefit driven advertising. Every product or service -- no matter how generic -- can advertise a benefit. Yes, soft drinks too! I can replace the above billboard with the following:

Driving is Tiring
Coke is Refreshing

QuikTrip Convenience Store
Exit 112 -- Now!

I've selected a specific audience. I've offered a clear benefit. I've even snuck in a Call-to-Action. Brilliant! (I might also include a mouth-watering image of a sweating bottle of Coke -- the right graphic device can communicate a benefit even faster than words). Coca-Cola actually used to advertise this way. I'd encourage them to test a quarter of their advertising budget (maybe a billion dollars or so) on it again.

Communicating effectively in the marketplace means identifying what motivates your target audience. Every product and service solves a problem or satisfies a need for someone. A good ad speaks in terms of solutions to problems. People are motivated by solutions.

Luxury items that "nobody needs" still satisfy emotional cravings. Even good image-advertising seeks to motivate us on a subconscious level by playing on our needs of belonging to a group or feeling important. Just look at clothing ads targeting teenagers.

What powerful compelling benefit can your company offer? Put it in words; be concise and specific; then run with it. The results will be amazing.

Question for discussion or continued thought:

What solution(s) does your business offer your customers?

CHAPTER THREE - FEAR

In this chapter, I find wisdom in understanding the motive power of some of our most basic emotions.

Fear is the most powerful motivator. It is primitive, and it is so strong that it even influences our "fun" motivations like desire.

I begin by telling of the first time I recall being frightened, and how fear leaves a lasting legacy. Later, in the chapter, we will look at how doubt, revenge, worry, shame, and anger, are all manifestations of fear; and how you can conquer them.

We will examine how fear keeps us from dealing with change and trying new things. Both of those require a comfort with risk. I will show you how you can become more comfortable with risk.

You will learn numerous techniques on how you can overcome the power of fear, and turn it to your advantage.

Robert Evans Wilson, Jr.

The Most Powerful Motivator

How fear is etched into our brains

I was abruptly awakened and told, "The house is on fire. Go outside!" As I ran out of my bedroom and into the hall my socks slipped on the polished oak floor. A guiding hand helped me keep my footing and a frantic voice urged, "Hurry! Hurry!"

As I got to the door I looked over my shoulder and saw flames leaping out of the heating grate on the floor. The door was thrown open and I was shoved outside into the carport. "Go stand in the driveway and wait for me. And, DO NOT come back inside. Do you hear me? DO NOT come back inside the house!"

The door shut and I began to cry. I stood and stared at the sea foam green door with the frosted jalousie windows. I waited and waited, but I did not go stand in the driveway. I couldn't move. I began to shiver as the cold concrete floor seeped through my socks, and the winter air penetrated my pajamas. It seemed to take forever, and with each passing minute, I cried harder. I could taste the salt of tears flowing down my face and into my mouth.

Finally the door reopened and my mother announced, "The fire is out." Relief flooded my body as I ran into her arms and she held me tight. I was two years old and the mental images of that day are as clear as if it happened yesterday. It is perhaps my oldest memory.

As an advertising and marketing consultant, I know there are many things that motivate us. During my presentations I frequently conduct straw polls, where I ask my audiences what motivates them. The first answers are usually about desires, but eventually someone remembers the most powerful motivator of all. FEAR.

Fear is a primal instinct that served us as cave dwellers and today. It keeps us alive, because if we survive a bad experience, we never forget how to avoid it in the future. Our most vivid memories are born in Fear. Adrenaline etches them into our brains.

Nothing makes us more uncomfortable than fear. And, we have so many: fear of pain, disease, injury, failure, not being accepted, missing an opportunity, and being scammed to name a few. Fear invokes the *flight or fight syndrome*; and our first reaction is always to flee back to our comfort zone. If we don't know the way back, we are likely to follow whoever shows us a path.

Wisdom in the Weirdest Places

Marketers use fear as a motivator as often as they can. They present a scenario they hope will invoke our sense of fear. Then they show us a solution – a path back to our comfort zone – that entails using their product or service. Fear is used to sell virtually everything: cars, tires, and life insurance are classics. But, clever marketers also use it to sell breakfast cereal and deodorant. As a result we purchase all sorts of things that a generation ago were considered unnecessary: antibacterial soap, alarm systems, vitamins... the list goes on and on.

Politicians will also use fear to motivate. They invoke fear of terrorism, threats to children's safety, etc. in order to pass new laws, get more votes, and to gain more power. As Rahm Emanuel, former Obama White House Chief of Staff, candidly admitted to the New York Times, "Rule 1: Never allow a crisis to go to waste. They are opportunities to do big things."

WARNING: Fear can be too powerful to use as a motivator because it can also paralyze - the classic *deer in the headlights syndrome*. Would you like to use fear to motivate your employees to perform better? "If you don't sell more widgets - you're FIRED!" It can work, but there are rules you must follow for it to be successful. To use fear successfully as a motivator, a solution must be offered with it. A new path to follow. You can tell an employee he or she must sell more, but unless you show them how, fear will cause flight or worse: paralysis.

Fear is a powerful motivator, but it is a negative one. I prefer to motivate someone by eliminating doubt. Doubt destroys motivation. If you can help a person get rid of it, you will motivate them positively. I will elaborate on this later in this chapter.

Question for discussion or continued thought:

What is your earliest memory? Is it connected to something that frightened you?

Change Please

*Motivation means you're either moving
toward or away from something*

"Security is mostly a superstition. It does not exist in nature, nor do the children of men as a whole experience it. Avoiding danger is no safer in the long run than outright exposure. Life is either a daring adventure, or nothing."

These are the words of the woman who became the poster child for overcoming adversity. A woman who was isolated into the two dimensional world of touch and smell at the age of 19 months. Yet, she went on to inspire millions around the world. Sightless and deaf, Helen Keller resolved to make something of her life. She lived with a keen understanding that change is inevitable, but growth is intentional. Unwilling to give in to her blindness, she chose to strive for a normal life.

Motivation is all about motion or movement. In other words, if you are comfortable, if you are happy and content, then you DO NOT move. You do not change. Why would you? On the other hand, if you are uncomfortable, if you're unhappy, then you want to change. You want to move back toward your comfort zone. There are millions of motivators in the world and all of us at any one time are being motivated by a dozen or more: Hunger, Safety, Sex, Love, Enlightenment to name just a few.

Interestingly, you can take all those motivators and boil them down to a variation of two basic emotions: Fear and Desire. You are either moving toward something you desire; or you are moving away from something you fear.

Fear, however, can become paralyzing and will keep us in one un-comfort zone because we fear the perceived discomfort that comes with change. We fear that change could open a Pandora's Box of more and scarier changes. I've seen it in relationships and in business.

I know a married couple who over the years have drifted apart and their marriage has become stagnant. I know they both desire greater intimacy with the other, but they both fear rejection and so they do nothing.

Wisdom in the Weirdest Places

I know a small business owner who watched his business shrink in the recent recession. His self-esteem is closely tied to his success and his falling income triggered fears of inadequacy. Frozen by fear into doing the same thing over and over again and expecting different results, he has not adapted to the changes going on in his market.

Helen Keller once again has wise words for such situations, "When one door of happiness closes, another opens; but often we look so long at the closed door that we do not see the one which has been opened for us."

When couples try new things together they actually stimulate the receptors in their brains that invoke the feelings of romance. Taking a class or starting a new hobby together is a great way for couples to renew their feelings for each other and discover a greater depth of intimacy.

For small business owners, a recession is a great time to try out a new idea or innovation. It attracts renewed interest in the business and can even create new customers and open new markets.

The trick is getting comfortable with change a little at a time. Start engaging in simple changes at home. Low risk changes will generate immediate rewards. Here are a few you can make that will help you get into a habit of adapting to change:

If you drink coffee every day, switch to tea for a week. If you always listen to rock music on the radio, switch to country, jazz, or classical for a week. Rearrange one piece of furniture in your house. Read a section of the newspaper that you've never read before. Take a continuing education class in a subject not related to your career. Join a hobby group on MeetUp.com. Taste an ethnic food that you've never tried before, (as an alternative revisit a food you think you hate).

Question for discussion or continued thought:

What are some low to medium risk changes that you can begin to make in your life now?

Robert Evans Wilson, Jr.

Defeating the De-Motivator

When seeds of doubt creep into consciousness

    The sweet strains of a Puccini aria cut through the Saturday night clatter of the busy Italian restaurant in New York City, but it wasn't coming from the aging voice of the Sicilian baritone who was hired to belt out favorites like *Funiculi-Funicula*. It was a soprano whose crystal clear voice filled the room. Within moments all the ambient noise came to a halt. Diners stopped eating and talking, busboys stopped clearing tables; the cooks even came out of the kitchen.
    Singing on the tiny stage was the skinny moon-faced waitress from Ohio. The Sicilian heard she studied opera, so he invited her to join him, but what began as a duet ended in solo as he too was mesmerized by the beauty of her voice. When she finished, the place thundered in applause and I saw tears of gratitude glistening in her eyes. She had hit each note perfectly.
    If only she had done that when she auditioned for the Metropolitan Opera. But she choked, flinched, allowed a seed of doubt to creep into her consciousness and thus her voice.
    She told me her story over a couple of beers after work. It was the fall of 1984, and I was a fellow waiter at the restaurant; just another struggling artist in the city that never sleeps. She explained that she got nervous during her audition and couldn't hit the high notes. She would get one more chance to audition, but she would have to wait an entire year.
    I never found out if she made it; as a writer my art is portable and a few months later I moved to a city where they still have a bedtime. I suspect she did, because that night she received a proof - a vital beginning step.
    Doubt is a silent killer. We transmit feelings of doubt to others through subtleties in our body language, facial expression and tone of voice. It is picked up subconsciously by those with whom we communicate. Worse than that, we communicate it to ourselves, and it seeps into our performance. Doubt is *the* De-Motivator and all too often it prevents us from even trying.
    We all suffer doubt occasionally, and its cure is always the same: proof. Proof that we are indeed talented enough to do what we

set out to do. A proof doesn't need to be big to eliminate doubt. A series of little ones can be just as effective.

I keep a journal – a log – of accomplishments. Both small and large, because they all add up to reasons for believing in my abilities. It is especially important to log the little ones, because they are so easy to forget or overlook, and yet they carry tremendous weight when it comes to giving ourselves confidence.

You say, "I'm just starting out and have no accomplishments." That just means you're not looking in the right places. We all have successes; some of them may be found in different areas of your life. I often read in the Wall Street Journal about women, who after years as stay-at-home Moms, return to the workforce in well-paid management positions. They acquire these jobs by citing in their resumes the many skills and achievements they learned through their volunteer work. What talents are you racking up through your hobbies and leisure activities?

Sometimes proof comes to us by comparing ourselves to others. Simply ask yourself, "Out of all the people who have ever lived, how many have attained what I want?" The sheer numbers alone will often be all the proof you need.

When all else fails, fall back on faith. Some of the most successful people in the world had absolutely no proof that they could achieve their dreams. All they had was a strong desire and a belief in themselves. As Martin Luther King, Jr. once said, "Take the first step in faith. You don't have to see the whole staircase, just take the first step."

Question for discussion or continued thought:

What accomplishments will you add to your log?

Robert Evans Wilson, Jr.

The Second Mouse Gets the Cheese

*It's the willingness to take risks
that defines the innovator*

My title this month is a funny metaphor for a common opinion that I found written on a bathroom wall. The understood part of the graffiti is that the first mouse must die springing the trap before the second one gets the prize.

After observing big failures, it's human nature to be a little wary of trying new things. Fear of failure tends to make us less likely to take risks even if we're not putting our lives in jeopardy. No one likes to lose money, or even lose face on an idea that doesn't work.

Another anonymous bathroom wall writer phrased the same sentiment this way: *Eagles may soar, but weasels are never sucked into airplane engines*. In short, many people are motivated by security. And, when I observe the differences between my two sons, I can see how it happens.

My first son, by virtue of birth order, had to be a trail blazer. He was first to play soccer, baseball and basketball, attend Cub Scouts and go to school. Meanwhile, my second son, forced to sit on the sidelines and watch, enjoyed all the benefits of seeing his big brother struggle, thus learning what to avoid. When his turn to try those things finally arrived, he was prepped and succeeded quickly and easily.

A second mouse rarely leaves his comfort zone. "Uh, go ahead... you try it first. I'll just stay over here in my safe cozy world and watch. If you don't die, and it looks like there's something to gain, then maybe I'll try it."

I think Mark Twain said it best, "A man with a new idea is a crank -- until the idea succeeds."

A desire for security, and its accompanying risk avoidance, keeps us from even testing our potential. I remember when I started my first advertising business, many of the writers and graphic designers I knew would say to me, "I wish I could be self-employed like you and have the freedom to set my own hours. If I could just find one client, I could quit my job."

I always responded by saying, "You're not going to find that client until you quit your job. There's nothing more motivating than

Wisdom in the Weirdest Places

a mortgage payment at the end of the month, to get you out there and find one. As long as you're comfortably receiving a steady paycheck, you're not going to take that risk."

More than any other characteristic, it is the willingness to take risks that defines the innovator. Today our sluggish economy is screaming for some innovation. Unfortunately, at the same time, our society is shunning risk like never before.

As we have become wealthier as a nation, we have become more comfortable and less risk tolerant. Meanwhile our government - always moving with the will of the people - has attempted to secure that comfort for us in the only way it knows how.

In the name of protecting people, our government has stepped up regulation on business to the point that it has stifled innovation. A certain amount of constraint stimulates creative thinking - that's where the term "thinking outside of the box" was derived. But, the increasing level of regulations and the accompanying penalties for violating them has upped the ante on risk.

According to *The Economist* magazine, "There are over 4,000 federal crimes, and many times that number of regulations that carry criminal penalties... many laws, especially federal ones, are so vaguely written that people cannot easily tell whether they have broken them."

When it is impossible to know the rules, it makes it even scarier to try something new that could possibly break them and land you in jail. Security is nice to have, but it is more about being ever vigilant than it is about finding a no-tolerance rule that will cover every exigency. Financial security, in particular, is tied to your mind, not your paycheck.

Benjamin Franklin warned us more than two hundred years ago, "They, who can give up essential liberty to obtain a little temporary safety, deserve neither liberty nor safety."

Innovation requires creative thinking, time, and the willingness to take risks. None of those matter if the environment to try new things is severely limited. Innovation also requires liberty - the freedom to fail or succeed.

For the sake of the economy, we need to give those First Mice, the ones willing to take risks, the freedom to try.

Question for discussion or continued thought:

When have you been a second mouse? When have you been a first mouse?

Wisdom in the Weirdest Places

Instead Of Serving It Cold... Don't Serve It at All

*Revenge is a survival instinct dating
back to our caveman days*

On a summer day in 1973, my 12 year old sister was riding her horse on the quiet streets near our house. There was a little more traffic than usual as two cars came toward her from opposite directions. Cindy rode onto the well-tended lawn of a stately two-story house to get out of the way. While she waited, her horse relieved himself. She then rode on, unknowing that her steed had left a pile of manure on the emerald zoysia grass.

Cindy was two hundred feet down the road, when a car sped past, then skidded to a tire-squealing halt in front of her horse. The startled horse reared up; throwing Cindy to the pavement below. A man leapt out of his car, then without asking if she was hurt, started screaming at her for allowing her horse to defecate on his lawn. Crying and in pain from bruises to her back and arms, Cindy struggled to her feet, and then managed to catch her horse who had only wandered off a few feet.

She apologized profusely, but the hysterical homeowner would not be satisfied. He insisted she walk her horse back to his yard, where he forced her to remove the horse droppings with her bare hands. Then without offering her an opportunity to wash her hands, he ordered her off his property.

I was enraged when she told me the story. As a hormone-filled sixteen year old, I wanted to retaliate on her behalf. I told her I would get two hundred pounds of salt; then under the cover of night, use it to write a message on his lawn. Within a few days, alphabet-shaped sections of his grass would die. Revenge would be sweet as his neighbors read in brown letters the profane words that described the true nature of his character.

Fortunately, my sister is more forgiving than me, and refused to tell me which house the jerk lived in. Cindy's wisdom probably kept me out of jail.

Revenge is anger in action; and anger is rooted in fear. When we are afraid, we will do almost anything to make that feeling go away.

Revenge is a powerful motivator. It is a survival instinct that dates back to our caveman days. If we were attacked and did not retaliate, then our enemy would attack again and again until they succeeded in killing us.

The problem is that when someone hurts us today, that primal urge still rises quickly. It doesn't take much - it can be an emotional injury, an insult or a rejection - to stimulate that response within us. That feeling is very powerful. If we act upon it, we usually find ourselves feeling worse than before the slight. And, if we get too carried away, we may find ourselves on the wrong side of the law. As Mahatma Gandhi observed, "An eye for an eye makes the whole world blind."

The trick is curbing that response, and using that powerful motivation in a positive way for ourselves. I like the way psychologist and author, Vijai P. Sharma, puts it, "It is better to let the other person get away with it, so that you can get away from it."

We can control our instinct and put it to work for us instead of against us by using that energy in positive ways. Exercise is a great way to blow off that initial steam you feel. I like to get out on my in-line skates and skate ten or more miles. Not only does it burn energy, the repetitive activity is meditative and allows me to put things into perspective.

Loving yourself by investing in your personal growth and development is another way to thwart those primal urges. Use your time to get better at what you do - pour that energy into your business and hobbies. Treat yourself to a massage, a gourmet meal, or a mini-vacation. And, surround yourself with friends who know and love you best. As Welsh poet, George Herbert, said in 1630, "Living well is the best revenge."

Question for discussion or continued thought:

Have you ever felt moved by revenge? Did you act on it, or did you find an alternative outlet for it?

Wisdom in the Weirdest Places

What's Keeping You Awake?

*Worry feels like motivation but it
is actually a de-motivator*

The other day on the radio I heard these lyrics from the Shinedown song, *If You Only Knew* "It's 4:03 and I can't sleep... I toss and turn like the sea." I thought, "Yeah, why is it always 4AM that I wake up when I'm worried about something?" The singer of this top 10 pop rock song was troubled by a woman. What's keeping you awake?

Most of us, at one time or another, have spent sleepless hours in bed worrying about something. Then making it worse, you're tired the whole next day.

Over the years, I've ruminated over all sorts of things. Big issues I have little or no control over like politics, the environment, terrorism, and the economy. Personal issues that I need to affect such as my business, my family, and my relationships. I have even worried over my volunteer work. Churning the same thoughts over and over again.

Some of us worry about the past - what could've been if only we had done something differently. Others worry about some future problem that hasn't even occurred yet.

Worry feels like motivation because it is rooted in the desire to fix a situation, but it is actually a de-motivator. It robs us of valuable energy we need to live a productive life. I love this modern update to an old proverb: "Worry is a brisk ride on a rocking horse; you burn a lot of energy, but you don't get anywhere." It is an amusing proverb that creates an accurate metaphor, but it does not offer us an answer on how to deal with worry.

For a simple solution on countering worry, I've always enjoyed the lyrics of this Irving Berlin song from the movie *White Christmas*:

*When I'm worried and I can't sleep,
I count my blessings instead of sheep;
and I fall asleep, counting my blessings.*

Although, I must admit that I didn't really hear these sage words or make use of them for years.

When I finally did; I found that it really works. Sometimes we have to start with the basics, and remind ourselves of all that we do have and all that is going smoothly in our lives in order to put the troubling matter into perspective: "I have a roof over my head, I have my health, I have food in the house, I have a car, I have friends, etc."

I recently revisited Dale Carnegie's book, *How to Stop Worrying and Start Living*. It was written during the Great Depression and World War II; a period of time when most people had plenty to stress over. The advice still holds up today.

The trick is to divert your pensive energy into practical projects. Carnegie suggests that we focus on doing our best one day at a time and the future will take care of itself. In other words, keep busy! Get so caught up in your work that you have no time to ponder all the "What ifs" that have been running like a broken record in your mind.

He also suggests that you ask yourself, "What is the worst that could happen?" Then he says to either accept that or seek out the answers you need to fix it. If you choose the later, you must collect all the facts, analyze them, make a decision, then act on it.

I think his best suggestion is to spend your time helping others. When you focus on what you can do for others, you cannot at the same time focus on yourself. Or in the words of one unknown author, "When you dig another out of their troubles, you find a place to bury your own."

Eventually you can utter the immortal words of *MAD Magazine*'s Alfred E. Neuman, "What, me worry?"

Question for discussion or continued thought:

What worries do you have? What can you do to fix them, or let them go?

Wisdom in the Weirdest Places

KA-BOOM! The Explosive Pain of Shame

Shame is so powerful it can make you feel worthless

Twelve years ago, I phoned a prospective client that I'd been courting for months. The last time we'd spoken, only a few weeks earlier, she expressed interest in my conducting a seminar for her company. This time she said, "I was in the audience at the Fox theatre last week; we won't be needing your services."

My face burned red with shame, as her words forced me to recall the most challenging experience I've ever had as a humorist.

It was my second year working as a presenter when I was hired to serve as the Master of Ceremonies for a landscape design association's award dinner. The job was easy enough, just read a description of what the recipient did to win the award, call them up to the stage, and give them a trophy. Grateful for the opportunity, and wanting to provide additional value to my service, I offered to open the program with a ten minute comedy routine. My client graciously accepted.

On the morning of the program, I woke up with the flu. I had a sore throat, congestion, 103 degree fever, chills and aches. I was miserable. Recalling the adage, "the show must go on," I dosed myself with the maximum allowed quantities of several over-the-counter medications. Throughout the day, I pumped myself up with chicken soup and hot tea. By show time, I was feeling pretty good.

I stepped onto the stage and told my first joke. To my shock no one laughed. So, I moved right onto my next one. Again, no one laughed. I'd never experienced this before and I started to feel a sense of panic. Nevertheless, I forged ahead and told joke number three. Silence! I couldn't understand it, I'd told these jokes dozens of times to dozens of audiences and they always laughed.

Joke number four fell flat. I was now in full panic, and at one point I couldn't even remember my next joke. I didn't know what to do. I didn't know how to recover. I plodded on hoping they would laugh at the next one. They never did. My throat became parched, and I had nothing to drink. With each un-laughed-at joke, my throat became dryer and more constricted until I could barely speak. I skipped to the end, and delivered my very best jokes... still nothing. I finally finished, and received no applause - not that I expected any at that point. The whole thing lasted only five minutes - the longest five minutes of my life.

Remarkably the rest of the program went without a hitch. I read the descriptions, gave out the awards and completed evening. Needless to say, I never wanted to experience the humiliation of bombing so badly again. On the other hand, I didn't want to give up delivering humorous presentations - the joy of making people laugh is wonderful. I was determined to discover what went wrong, and how I could fix it.

In hindsight, I could see that my timing was off. I could easily blame that on being sick, but the real problem was that I didn't have the experience or know-how to turn it around. The first thing I did was make sure I always had a glass of water. The second thing I did was talk to several comedians and humorists to learn what they did when a joke bombed. Before long I had the answers I needed.

Now, when a joke tanks I make fun of it. First by making a whistling sound of a bomb dropping followed by the sound of explosion, then I say, "Whew, that joke didn't just bomb - it stunk!" I, then, wave the air where I was standing as if to blow away the smell, while stepping away from that spot dramatically as if the area, itself, was contaminated by nuclear fallout. That almost always gets a laugh. It also humanizes me in the eyes of the audience; I'm fallible and can make light of it. Usually the very next joke I tell will get a laugh, if only out of sympathy. I've learned many other techniques and as a result I haven't bombed since.

I was motivated by shame, one of the worst feelings an individual can have. I never wanted to feel that again.

People confuse shame, guilt and embarrassment because they are very similar feelings, but the roots of these feelings are very different. We experience embarrassment, when we accidentally make a mistake such as spilling a drink down the front of our shirts. We suffer guilt, when we do something we know is wrong. Shame, however, is born of ignorance or of not having mastered a concept - such a social behavior - that we think we have mastered.

We feel shame when we are unexpectedly condemned or criticized for something we didn't know is incorrect. The shame comes when we recognize the obviousness of our error. It makes us feel stupid. If we know in advance that it is incorrect, the feeling we experience instead is guilt or embarrassment.

Wisdom in the Weirdest Places

I recall being shamed by my classmates in elementary school when I shared a belief that women get pregnant by kissing. Hey, I came by it honestly! Remember that little song, "Johnny and Suzy sitting in tree, K-I-S-S-I-N-G. First comes love, then comes marriage, then comes Johnny with a baby carriage."

So, if shame was such an effective motivator for me, would I recommend using it to motivate others? ABSOLUTELY NOT! Shame is extremely motivating when it comes to eliminating unwanted behavior, but at the same time it is also a de-motivator. Shame is so powerful, it can make someone feel worthless and completely shut them down. Shame hits like a fist, and when it comes during childhood, some people spend the rest of their lives trying to recover from it.

Motivate instead with understanding and kind explanation.

Question for discussion or continued thought:

When have you felt shame? Did it motivate you or shut you down?

Robert Evans Wilson, Jr.

Deadlines Work

Put yourself in a box in order to think outside of it

As I sit here writing this article against the deadline; I'm reminded of my days as a young advertising copywriter when I occasionally needed a deadline as motivation to finish a boring project. The deadline did more than motivate me to finish -- more often than not, it was what finally stimulated enough creative thinking to move me forward -- in other words, it motivated me to think outside of the box.

"Thinking outside of the box." Boy, has that phrase become overused. People are so often telling us that we need to think outside of the box that it has fallen into the realm of cliché. Nevertheless it is still true. Sometimes, however, we need to be put into a box first before we can think outside of it. A deadline is just such a box.

I used to believe that the more freedom I had the more creative I could be. But it doesn't necessarily work that way. Ingenuity needs to be motivated by something, and if the desire to achieve isn't there, then an uncomfortable boundary may work.

Have you ever watched a man or a woman with one leg running a marathon or competing in downhill snow skiing? I have, and every time I'm deeply impressed because I have both of my legs and I can't do either one. I used to wonder why they were able to do so much more than me when I was the one born with the greater advantage. Now I can see that the difference is that they were challenged by a boundary and I wasn't. Some of them might even argue that they were the ones born with the greater advantage. Being unable to walk made them uncomfortable, and conquering their disability became a powerful motivating factor. They had to get out of that box!

Think of creativity as a prisoner trying to bust out of jail. When your resources and opportunities are limited you must become innovative. A good illustration of this is the World War II movie *The Great Escape*. It is an amazing tale of ingenuity. Men with little to work with escape from a German POW camp. In addition to digging three tunnels without shovels, they made hand drawn traveling documents and identification papers that looked authentic enough to

Wisdom in the Weirdest Places

pass for ones made on a printing press. Now that was a box to get out of!

I have enjoyed working for myself most of my adult life. People frequently tell me they wish they could be self-employed like I am. They say things like, "If I could just get one client then I could quit my job." My response is always the same, "Until you quit your job, you are never going to find that first client. There is nothing like the deadline of a rent or mortgage payment staring you down at the end of the month to motivate you to get out and look for clients."

Everyone works under some kind of deadline. They force us to prioritize our responsibilities; they limit procrastination; and they help us achieve our work related goals. But, we often lack them in our private lives. We are not given deadlines to accomplish our most important personal goals and without those boundaries procrastination can creep in and destroy our best intentions. The trick is to impose a deadline on yourself. But it has to have some teeth to work.

Here's how to do it: Write down your goal. Then set a reasonable date in which you can achieve it. Next, go to your bank or attorney and set up an escrow account. Now add the teeth -- put into the account an amount of money that will hurt to lose: $1,000... $10,000... $100,000... You decide! Set it up so that if you haven't achieved your goal by the deadline then the funds go to a favorite charity... or make it even more motivating: let the funds go to your worst enemy!

Not ready to try that? Then try the buddy system. Pair up with a friend and each of you takes responsibility to follow up on the other one. You can get together once a week and check on each other's progress. If goals aren't being met, then nag each other into the uncomfort zone!

Question for discussion or continued thought:

Are you procrastinating over a particular task? Would a deadline help you finish it?

CHAPTER FOUR – STATUS AND PRESTIGE

In this chapter, it is my dog who grants me wisdom, along with my Mom, and a reader who challenged me to more deeply explore the motive power of social standing.

So, you don't think you're motivated by status? What kind of car do you drive? What neighborhood do you live in? How much money do you make? How many degrees and titles do you have? What awards have you won? What is your skill level in a particular sport, game, or profession?

How much do you give to charity, and to which ones? What kind of ballpoint pen do you carry? What kind of jacket do you wear? Do you have a prominent gold-capped tooth? Do you have a tattoo? What breed of dog do you own? There are so many ways in which we achieve and display status.

When someone tells you that they are not motivated by status or its symbols, call them on it. We will look at how status and prestige motivates people at all levels of society.

With three articles I will show you how status motivates us, and when it stops. We will look at how we are concerned with the way others perceive us, and how they set the bar for us. And, how when we reach the highest levels of status, we start giving back.

Robert Evans Wilson, Jr.

Pack Mentality

Humans are as motivated by status as pack animals

When my son was two years old, we got a Samoyed puppy, and for the next 18 months they were the best of friends. Then the dog changed. Suddenly she started growling at my son and biting him. At first I thought that maybe he was pulling her tail or something else that was irritating her, but that wasn't it.

My dog had become an adult and instinct kicked in. She became concerned with her place in the pack hierarchy. I learned that our family was her pack, that I was alpha-dog, and that she had no intention of being at the bottom of the pecking order. That meant someone had to be beneath her and the easiest choice was my toddler.

Through training and discipline we got the biting to stop, but to this day she still considers my son subordinate to her.

It's all about status and exclusivity. And human beings are just as motivated by it as a pack animal. When Abraham Maslow created his *Theory of Human Motivation* in 1943, he identified five levels of motivation or five needs that humans strive to satisfy. Those needs are, in order: Survival, Safety, Social, Esteem, and Fulfillment.

Status is an esteem need and regardless of where we fall on the economic ladder, we all strive to achieve status before we can move on to the highest need. Whether we admit it or not, we all want to feel as if we are a little bit better than the people around us. We begin to establish that - at least in our own minds - with the accouterments of wealth such as branded clothing, jewelry, luxury automobiles, and exclusive neighborhoods. Even the poorest of people find symbols with which to establish their status. The visibility of these status symbols can create the powerfully motivating emotion of envy.

Most happiness that is acquired by achieving status symbols is short lived. Overtime such trappings become meaningless to us, at which point, we seek genuine achievements to prove our worth. Studies have shown that after reaching a certain income level (usually around $250,000 a year) an individual's happiness does not increase until they reach the status of super rich (approximately $10,000,000 a year).

But, status can continue to motivate us long after money ceases to do so. Bestowing a new title with added responsibilities yet without any added pay is a common method for rewarding employees.

Volunteers can be motivated in a similar fashion. I was an adult Boy Scout leader for five years. The *Boy Scouts of America* rewards its leaders with patches embroidered with colorful square knots that are worn on the adult uniform. Different colored square knots represent the variety of services a volunteer has provided or achievements that he or she has earned. Some square knots represent achievements earned years earlier when the volunteer was a Boy Scout. When I attend formal full uniform functions, I find myself scanning fellow leaders' square knots to note their status. There is one we all look for; it is the red, white and blue knot that indicates the wearer earned the highest status in scouting as a youth: the Eagle Scout award.

When the United States was founded, one of its distinguishing characteristics from the rest of the world was the lack of a feudal or caste system. That doesn't mean status doesn't exist in America. Indeed it does, but here we must earn it. Best of all, people have a choice and can rise above the station they were born into.

Lacking status puts us in the un-comfort zone and drives us to achieve. When you help someone up the social ladder, you can motivate them in a powerful and positive way.

Question for discussion or continued thought:

What status symbols motivate you or still have the power to make you happy or proud?

Robert Evans Wilson, Jr.

You'll Know When You've Arrived

Are status symbols behind you? Probably not!

    During the 1996 Summer Olympics, I saw a young athlete with his brand new silver medal around his neck and a massive smile on his face. He was so thrilled with his achievement that he was mixing and mingling with everyone he met on the sidewalk. Perfect strangers were shaking his hand, slapping him on the back, and having their picture taken with him. I did not know who he was, but it was clear that he was relishing the highest point of his life to date.

    On March 29, 1982, amid thunderous applause, Katherine Hepburn stepped onto the stage at the Academy Awards to receive the Best Actress Oscar for her performance in *On Golden Pond*. Was she as thrilled as the Olympic athlete that I saw? Probably not. It was her fourth. Been there, done that, the mantle is getting crowded.

    In my previous article, *Pack Mentality*, I wrote that human beings are highly motivated by status and its symbols. A reader contacted me and said she had grown beyond that. She told me how, after 20 years of financial success, she put the corporate world and materialism behind her. She now works at a fraction of her previous earnings for a non-profit organization dedicated to enhancing the lives of babies.

    I agreed that she had put status and its symbols behind her, but only in one area of her life. I then asked her what level of comfort she was seeking to achieve in her new career.

    Abraham Maslow, in his *Theory of Human Motivation*, identified five levels of need that people strive to satisfy (in order, they are: Survival, Safety, Social, Esteem, and Fulfillment). I have found that we work through those five levels separately in each area of our lives: work, relationships, parenting, hobbies, sports, volunteering, etc. With each new endeavor, we attempt to pass all the mileposts until we reach our comfort zone.

    There is a joke about parenthood that illustrates this: When the first baby drops her pacifier on the ground, the parents sterilize it before giving it back; with the second baby, the pacifier gets wiped off; and with number three, it just gets popped back into his mouth. I used to think the humor referred to how harried the parent was from

Wisdom in the Weirdest Places

handling the needs of three kids, but now I realize it refers to the parent's comfort level with raising children.

Status is an esteem need, and the symbols that accompany it are recognition for our achievements. However, as long as those status symbols remain important to us, then we haven't mastered that area of our lives. It is when we are in our comfort zone that the achievement is secure. At that point, the symbols are no longer important and we are ready to move on to the highest level: fulfillment. You will know you have reached the peak when you freely share your expertise with people who are levels below you.

Many years ago, I heard an interview with a professional football quarterback. The reporter asked him if he ever taught his secrets of success to younger up and coming players. He replied, "What, and lose my job to one of them? Hell no! Let them learn it on their own the way I did." Clearly, he was not yet in his comfort zone.

All of us have reached a comfort zone in one or more areas of our lives. I spent six years as a member of the public speaking organization, *Toastmasters International*. For the first four years, I was fully focused on learning and achieving. In that time, I completed two educational levels and won 13 speaking contests. During my last two years in Toastmasters, I became a professional speaker and was no longer interested in entering the contests. The shine of those "amateur" trophies had worn off a bit, and I found my joy was in sharing what I already knew with those who were just beginning.

You will know you have reached the highest level, when sharing your expertise is as satisfying as achievement.

Question for discussion or continued thought:

How are you sharing your expertise with someone who needs to learn it?

Robert Evans Wilson, Jr.

Good Habit - Questionable Motive

Exposing yourself to new things creates opportunity

I would like to share with you a story about my mom, a woman who was very insecure about her background. She grew up in a blue collar family where neither her mother nor father finished eighth grade. Mom completed high school, but only with tutoring by my father. She would frequently say to me, "I was born on the wrong side of the tracks."

At age 19, she married my father, the handsome son from a wealthy family. Her beauty and charm trumped all the debutantes in town, and swept Dad off his feet. She thought she had it made and that all her fears would go away. Money and position, however, would not erase her feelings of inferiority. Those feelings were intensified instead. The contrast between her education and her in-laws with professional degrees was intimidating.

Mom wanted to fit in, join the discussions, and be an authority in her own right. In short, she wanted to feel important in her new family, and she realized that she needed more knowledge. Determined to find a way to reduce her education deficit, Mom threw herself into reading.

Any subject appealed to her at first, and over time she found her favorites and pursued them to excellence. One thing she had no time for was fiction.

It was a habit that served her well, and in 1960 paid off in a big way. That year my dad was diagnosed with kidney failure and given less than a year to live. There was no cure, and my parents were advised to start planning for the day he would die.

Three years old at the time, my recollections are that my strong Daddy could no longer pick me up and carry me. That he did not go to work very often, and spent his days in bed. I noticed Mom took over all the driving and occasionally pulled off the road so Dad could vomit.

Mom and Dad sold their house and used the proceeds to buy a four-unit apartment house with the plan that Mom, my sister and I would live in one unit and live off the rents of the other three. The plan was for my mother to work part time until my sister and I were

Wisdom in the Weirdest Places

old enough for school, then she would work full time. Until Dad's illness, she had been a stay home Mom.

After high school, Mom trained as an x-ray technician, but had not worked in years. She began to take temp jobs to beef up her skills and to develop a network of potential employers when the inevitable day arrived.

At one of those early temp jobs, the x-ray machine broke. An extended period of down time ensued, and Mom went to the magazine rack in the doctor's lobby for something to read. She passed over the popular magazines of the day after finding an out of date medical journal. "This looks like something good for my mind!" she thought.

In an article about physicians in Boston conducting experimental surgery, she learned of the world's first kidney transplants. At the time of the writing, the doctors were looking for volunteers. Her pulse quickened. As she read on, she discovered there was a prerequisite. The volunteers had to have an identical twin. Dad happened to have an identical twin.

At that point Mom ran to the nearest phone and dialed Boston until she got one of those doctors on the line. "Yes," he replied, "we are still looking for volunteers. Send me your husband and his brother." That night they went to visit my Uncle Ralph, who said, "To save your life, absolutely yes, you may have one of my kidneys."

I share this story because Mom developed a lifelong habit of reading non-fiction because she wanted to impress her in-laws and other people who intimidated her. In the end, her habit saved my dad's life. He became the 12th person in the world to have a kidney transplant and live. And, I got Dad for 18 more years.

My mom may have been motivated by her fears, but it is a fact of life that when you expose yourself to new things you will recognize opportunities that others will miss. So, pick up a book, take a class, or visit a new place and see what exciting things open up for you.

Question for discussion or continued thought:

What new things and experiences are you exposing yourself to?

CHAPTER FIVE - CONNECTION

In this chapter, I find wisdom in laughter, in attempting to be "cool," in playing football for the wrong reasons, and from being foolish in love.

What would we be without friends and family? Relationships are the most important thing in most people's lives. How we are connected to others, and how we achieve those connections are highly motivating.

One of the top regrets of people who are dying is not having kept in touch with family and friends. According to Daniel Gilbert, psychology professor at Harvard University, and happiness expert: "We are happy when we have family, we are happy when we have friends and almost all the other things we think make us happy are actually just ways of getting more family and friends."

I begin by sharing how "making friends" was a skill that came slowly for me. In the following articles, we will look at how relationships develop. And, why it is so important to remain true to our own beliefs and desires.

We will examine how drama triangles create tension and unhappiness in relationships.

We will also look at relationship tools like humor and vulnerability. How they enhance our connections with people, and how they help us motivate others.

Finally, we will look at how forgotten events in our past can continue to motivate us in the present.

Robert Evans Wilson, Jr.

Craving Connection

*We desire relationships because
they make us feel important*

    I was walking home from school when Gary, a kid from my third grade class, fell in beside me and started chatting. I'd never spoken with him before, and I had no idea why he was talking to me, but I enjoyed it. Here was someone, whom I did not know, who was interested in me - it was a new experience and it felt good. We said goodbye at his house which was about halfway to mine. He walked with me again the next day; and the day after that. On the third day, he asked me if I wanted to come into his house and play. I called my mother from his home phone and she said it was okay.

    He was the first friend I'd made on my own without my parents arranging it. Of course, Gary had done all the work. He initiated contact, he started the first conversation, he then had an effective transition question to move us to the next level. Gary had social skills and courage that I did not have. We became best friends for next three years until my family moved to a new neighborhood.

    Unfortunately, I didn't learn many of Gary's skills, and found myself isolated once again in the new neighborhood. Oh, there were plenty of kids around, but they all seemed to have their own friends, and I was too afraid to approach them. One day, Steve, another new kid in the area found me and struck up a conversation. He too, had social skills that I lacked - including a transition question: "Do you want to "hang out" at my house?"

    Over the next several weeks Steve and I spent a lot of time together, but he made me uncomfortable. I ignored those feelings because my hunger for connection was a stronger motivator than my fear of trouble. Steve used stronger profanity than I was used to. He stole cigarettes from his mother, and copies of *Playboy* magazine from his father. He stuck out his thumb to hitchhike when we walked to the store, and if someone stopped he got into their car. Worst of all, he enjoyed vandalism and threw rocks to break windows in houses that were under construction. And, he talked me into joining him in all of that. Our brief friendship lasted until our parents caught us doing one of those things, and forbade us from seeing each other again. I learned that I needed to be more choosey when accepting

Wisdom in the Weirdest Places

friendships, but I still hadn't figured out how to create one. In the meantime, I was miserably lonely.

I would make my first best friend in high school purely by accident. Tony and I walked into class one day wearing the same garish outfit: red jeans and a white shirt with red stripes and roses (hey, it was the 1970s!). Not only were we dressed alike, but we looked similar enough that people often thought we were brothers. The kids in class immediately started calling us the *Bobbsey Twins* which made us cringe in shame. We had two more classes together, so Tony suggested we cut school for the rest of the day. We did and hid out at his house.

I made my next several friends just by hanging out with Tony. He was a people magnet; he was gregarious, funny, and lived on the edge. His charisma attracted an array of satellites - one of whom became my next best friend. Dick and I were alike in many ways and developed a friendship that exists to this day (that is if he doesn't read this and see that I called him a satellite).

By the time I reached the end of high school I had some passable skills for making friends, but it wouldn't be until adulthood that I learned the simple lessons Gary knew as a young boy.

We live for human connection. We greatly desire relationships because they increase our confidence and self-esteem. They make us feel important, worthy, and good enough. We are motivated by those powerful feelings to develop social skills so that we can meet people and develop friendships.

Personally, I've craved connection so strongly that I have occasionally ignored "red flags" and made bad choices of those I've allowed to get close to me. The consequences never landed me in jail, but they did come close a few times.

Once we've broken the ice and made a few friends, we are motivated to refine those skills. We become more discriminating and find people who better match our values and personality.

Question for discussion or continued thought:

How has human connection enriched your life?

Robert Evans Wilson, Jr.

Lubricate with Laughter

*There's integrity in humor because
true laughter can't be forced*

    I was three or four jokes into my routine, when I realized that one of the troublemakers my client warned me about was sitting dead center on the front row. With arms firmly crossed over his chest, and a frown deeply embedded in his face, he was glaring defiantly at me with eyes that said, "You'll never make me laugh." In my mind, I silently agreed by nicknaming him: Stoneface.
    It was the beginning of a full day seminar on creativity in advertising. The meeting planner warned me that several members of the audience resented being forced to attend these workshops. She said they had caused problems for previous presenters - including heckling them!
    As a humorist, I'd long ago learned about the bonding nature of laughter, so I suggested that I open with a ten to fifteen minute comedy routine. I hoped that my humor would break the ice with the group, while signaling that it was going to be a fun day.
    It was a risk; even if there were no disrupters in the audience. Eight o'clock is early in the morning for comedy - especially if the coffee hasn't kicked in! Also stacked against me was an audience that was more than 75% male. Women laugh quicker and easier than men, plus their laughter incites the men to join in.
    While it started out slow, the laughter was growing steadily with each joke, but Stoneface was beginning to seem like an obstacle. I tried not to notice him, and simply work the audience on either side of him, but he was a very large man - both big and tall. He was an imposing figure that was difficult to ignore - and he became the challenge I wanted to overcome. Like most comedians, I have a *hip pocket joke* guaranteed to get a laugh if I start to bomb, but I left it out and continued to work my routine.
    He was winning, I was nearing the end of my opening, and his hostile stare had not let up one bit. At that point I found myself delivering the jokes directly to him - an act that did not go unnoticed by the rest of the audience. With each joke I served up, he held firm; yet the crowd around him was now roaring. I should have been satisfied, but I wasn't.

Wisdom in the Weirdest Places

Then it finally happened; I reached him with a surprise-ending, one-liner that split his face wide open. It was only a smile - he didn't even make a sound - but I couldn't resist pointing at him and saying, "Gotcha!" At that he laughed aloud - as did the entire audience - and in that moment we all bonded. Stoneface, who was now, Jim, became one of the most active participants that day.

I have often heard that it is impossible to hate someone who makes you laugh. Laughter is a bonding agent that we experience initially as babies when we develop our very first relationships - the ones with our parents; and it continues to be the social lubricant which enables us to make friends throughout our lives. French philosopher, Henri Bergson, said that laughter makes social life possible for human beings.

Because of its ability to bring people together, laughter can be a powerful motivational tool. But, you can't make someone laugh unless you are relating to them on a personal level. There is an integrity in humor because true laughter, like crying, cannot be forced. You must have empathy for your audience's frustrations and fears. And, you must inspire their trust.

While laughter is universal across the human species; humor is not. Jerry Seinfeld demonstrates this in an *American Express* commercial where the American slang in his stand up routine bombs in England because he doesn't understand the cultural nuances of the language. To stimulate laughter, you must find the common ground between you and your audience.

The broader the audience, the less subtle you can be with your humor. That is why silent movie slap-stick comedy so easily crossed international boundaries. Everyone can relate to the pain of Charlie Chaplin's character, *Little Tramp*, who despite having fallen on hard times, tries to maintain his gentlemanly dignity while dealing with bullying authority figures.

When you find a comic connection, laughter can be contagious... which reminds me of the "Laughing Quadruplet Babies" from *America's Funniest Videos*. If you haven't seen this, look it up on YouTube, and you'll find you can't help but laugh along.

We enjoy laughter so much because it makes us feel good. It is so powerful that it relieves stress and relaxes the entire body. It triggers the release of endorphins which can ease physical pain. It decreases stress hormones and boosts the immune system. While we are laughing we forget our fears, anxiety, and other discomforts. What can be better than that?

Share a laugh whenever you can. There are funny things to laugh about everywhere. As I was leaving the gym the other day, I saw a woman drinking Smartwater®. I pointed to the bottle and said, "I tried that once, but it didn't work." Then I quickly smacked the heel of my palm against my forehead, and shrugged. She laughed, so I grinned and added, "I must have drunk Smart-Ass Water by mistake." She laughed once more. Hmmm, maybe it's time for me to try stand-up again.

Question for discussion or continued thought:

How can you share some laughter at your place of work?

Wisdom in the Weirdest Places

How Cool are You?

What is it that really makes someone cool?

My sons recently started talking about being cool, and I recalled my own teenage years and the need to be *cool*. That driving desire dictated the clothes I wore, the music I listened to, and what subjects I became conversant in. And, yet despite all my motivation and effort, it remained elusive.

When I look back, I can see that all I really wanted was to be accepted, liked and admired. But, whatever I tried, I never quite felt *cool* enough. The problem was that I didn't really understand the term until I'd spent a few years living and working in the real world.

So, I explained to my kids, "*Cool* is when there's a problem and you do not get upset by it. When everyone else is panicking, rushing around and over reacting, the *cool* person is the one who stays calm, assesses the situation, then makes a reasoned decision on what to do."

One day, I'll tell them about Frances Healan, my friend who completely owned this concept. Mrs. Healan walked with a limp, and I learned that she had a severe condition or injury that could deteriorate and prevent her from ever walking again. That diagnosis was simply unacceptable to her. She had three daughters and two sons, all less than two years apart, with whom she had to keep up. Instead she ignored the pain and struggled to maintain the ability to walk under her own power. I never once knew her to mention the pain she continued to endure.

I met her when my friend Tony started dating Becky, the wildest of her children, and I dated Becky's best friend. It was while Tony and I waited for our dates to get ready, that I learned what an amazing conversationalist Mrs. Healan was. She would talk of her family and friends, of movies and novels. Pleasant stories that had no impact on my life or the world, and yet they were irresistibly soothing and peaceful. Meanwhile, with five rambunctious kids and their friends, hers was the house on the street where everything happened. It was a tumultuous environment of laughter one moment and tears the next as young personalities came together then clashed. Nothing ever seemed to rattle Mrs. Healan; she was always calm and relaxed.

Tony and Becky didn't last very long, but I refused to give up those wonderful conversations and started showing up just to hang out. Over the years, I realized that whenever my own life got a little stressed, I was drawn to the Healan household. Once there I would just sit and listen to Mrs. Healan's stories and absorb her serene energy. I was rejuvenated by her presence.

I never planned any of those visits. I would just start to feel the need, and before I knew it, was in the car driving. Those visits continued for years. Eventually the cumulative responsibilities of work, marriage and children made my life too busy for the simple pleasure of spending an afternoon with Mrs. Healan.

A few years ago she died of lung cancer. Frances was never a smoker, but a critical spot on her lung was missed on a routine chest x-ray. Her oncologist said that if he'd seen the x-ray when it was taken he could have saved her life. Despite that Frances Healan was never bitter.

Even though I had not seen her in years, her children called me to visit on her last day. When I arrived, her daughter Judy said, "Look Mama, it's Bobby Wilson." Mrs. Healan raised her head and said, "Bobby Wilson! Who's dying?" We all laughed. That moment sums up her life for me. Facing death she maintained her sense of humor. She was quite simply the coolest person I've ever known.

Question for discussion or continued thought:

What fashions or interests have you pursued in developing your public image?

Wisdom in the Weirdest Places

Facebook Drama Triangle

Storming in on a white horse can cost you a friend

Recently I posted an article on *Facebook* about a high school kid who was punished severely for something I considered to be a minor infraction. My friend, Jay, posted that he thought the kid deserved the punishment. Another friend, Pat, then posted, "Jay, you're an ass!" (I have changed my friends' names to protect their privacy).

I was disturbed by Pat's post, so I deleted it, and emailed him privately asking him to challenge Jay's assumptions and arguments, but to avoid name calling. He wrote me back telling me that I was spineless for trying to make everyone play nice in the sandbox. Then he unfriended me on *Facebook*.

Now, I have been friends with both of these men for more than 40 years. So, I was shocked that Pat unfriended me. I thought I was just encouraging some healthy debate, but on closer examination of my motives, I realize that I was trying to protect Jay. I created a drama triangle casting Jay as the *Victim*, Pat as the *Villain*, and myself as the *Hero* (ironically, Jay probably doesn't even know he was a victim because I most likely deleted the post before he had a chance to see it). In hindsight, I should have simply stayed out of it, and Pat would still be my friend.

The traditional drama triangle refers to the three roles as victim, persecutor, and rescuer. I have a rich history of being a rescuer. I recall fixing things around an ex-girlfriend's house that she had shown no interest in fixing, nor had she asked me to fix them; then I was disappointed when she showed little or no appreciation for the work I had done (thus casting myself into the role of victim).

I am guilty of being a helicopter parent trying to spare my children from the trials and pains of life. My sons finally asked me to stop helping them unless they asked for it (smart kids!).

As a 25 year old, I was proud of myself for rescuing my ex-wife from the filth and crime of New York City by moving her to Atlanta (she did want this). Yet by doing this, and several other rescues, she came to expect me to always satisfy her needs - often at the expense of mine.

Even my *Facebook* post was an attempt to rescue (from afar), the kid who was punished, by bringing attention to his plight.

In my defense, I came by my rescuer personality honestly. My mother, a narcissist, was always creating drama triangles from which I was expected to save her. Someone would "hurt her feelings" and I would assure her that I loved her unconditionally to make her "feel better." This is what I learned growing up, and it is a pattern that I have followed religiously.

I was unaware of the concept of drama triangles until I began therapy a few years ago. My therapist explained it to me, but I was resistant at first. I liked being a rescuer - I like helping people. I enjoy sharing what I have learned: showing elementary school kids how to deal with bullies; showing business owners how to increase sales with advertising; showing people how to think more creatively; and so on.

The trick is learning when people actually want my help, and whether or not it is really needed. I need to pause and determine if the situation is a drama triangle in the making - then stay the hell off of it!

It's time for me to retire my white hat, before I lose any more friends.

Question for discussion or continued thought:

How often do you find yourself in a drama triangle? Are you typically the victim, the rescuer, or the persecutor?

Wisdom in the Weirdest Places

The Victory of Vulnerability

Rolling over can be amazingly powerful

"Turn to chapter ten and begin reading..." My history teacher, by ending that sentence with a soft pause, led us to believe there were further instructions coming. The entire class stared at him in anticipation.

After a moment he said, "Why aren't you reading? Why are you looking at my face? There is no print here, and even if there was you couldn't see it."

The class burst into laughter. Frank Biggs, one of five African-American teachers in an all-white high school, frequently made fun of his race. He was a master of the self-deprecating joke, and subsequently the most popular teacher on campus.

In contrast to my comical teacher, I was clueless about the art of self-effacing humor, but I worked hard at cracking jokes and building a reputation as a class clown.

One day, after opening with his usual bit of comedy, Mr. Biggs asked the class, "Why is Africa called the Dark Continent?"

Wanting to compete with my entertaining teacher, I blurted out an answer I thought was certain to be rewarded with laughter from all: "Because of all the darkies that live there!"

Oops! The class laughed, but not Mr. Biggs. Instead, he spent the rest of the class scolding me for my insensitivity. He made me feel shame - that burning sensation of unworthiness - that most of us avoid at all costs. He also gave me a failing grade in Conduct for the semester. It was a grade that would keep me out of the Beta Club, an exclusive organization for high-achieving students, and limit my prospects for college. It was a high price to pay for creating a cool persona.

I was reluctant to tell this story - even though I was a high school kid and that was a different era, it seemed risky because it may be perceived differently today - but then I thought, "If I'm going to write advice about vulnerability, then I should be willing to live it as well."

Earlier in this chapter in my article: *Craving Connection*, I wrote about the universal craving for connection, and how we live for our friendships. Yet, at the same time, most of us repel the very intimacy we desire from our relationships. We do this by hiding our vulnerability, by building impervious walls - personas - to protect us from embarrassment and shame. Most of this emotional armor dates back to our early youth when we were terrified by a pimple, a bad-hair day, or wearing the wrong clothes.

Back in the 1970s, my friends and I would watch the TV show *Happy Days*. We all wanted to be cool like the leather-jacket clad, motorcycle riding, Fonzie. But it's easier to be funny than it is to be Fonzie, so I hid behind a shield of humor.

For the most part it worked. I made the other kids laugh and that made me cool. I was content. It would be decades before I learned the subtle art of making fun of myself in ways that people can relate to on a personal level.

American novelist, Madeleine L'Engle, notes, "When we were children, we used to think that when we were grown-up we would no longer be vulnerable. But to grow up is to accept vulnerability."

The truth is that we're terrified of making ourselves vulnerable because we are terrified of shame. So much so, that many of us have experienced nightmares of being naked or in our underwear in school or at work.

Eventually, I discovered and studied the wit of Woody Allen, who dead-panned his vulnerability, "I sold the memoirs of my sex life to a publisher. They are going to make a board game out of it."

When I started dating again after my divorce, I learned to turn the humor back on myself when I was asked potentially embarrassing questions that made me nervous. I recall responding to: "Do you like to dance?" with: "I love to dance... but I'm afraid the only step I know is the *Fred Flintstone*."

Over time, however, I began to notice that my relationships were as shallow as my jokes. I began to crave greater intimacy with my girlfriend, but I would expect her to be vulnerable - not me. Gee, why would I think that should be reciprocal?

Now, I'm finally beginning to figure out the power of vulnerability. When you show someone your true self, you invite trust. Why does this work? It works because people understand that we are risking shame and they completely relate to that.

It's not just for personal relationships; it works in business as well. I am comfortable standing on a stage speaking to hundreds or thousands of people, but talking with a client one-on-one for the first time scares the heck out of me. When I'm nervous, I become a chatterbox and talk non-stop, and while that serves me well on the platform, it is annoying in a conversation. I now explain this fear to my prospective clients, then ask them to tell me to put on the brakes if I get too talkative, and let me know it is their turn to speak. It's funny, but it seems to be happening less often – go figure!

Dr. Brene Brown, a professor of Social Work at the University of Houston, has labeled those who are willing to be vulnerable as "Whole-Hearted People." She identifies their number one trait as having the "courage to be imperfect."

Vulnerability is disarming, and makes aggressors back down. It is the primary component of *Verbal Judo* which I mention in Chapter Six: *Keep Your Power*.

Even dogs get it. When two dogs are fighting for hierarchy in a pack, one will eventually back down by rolling over and exposing his throat and belly. That act of vulnerability sends a powerful signal that keeps one dog from killing the other.

So, am I getting it? I looked at my website and my *Facebook* profile just before writing this, and noticed that I'm clearly still trying to be cool. On the other hand, I have found that the more vulnerable I am with the articles in my column the more favorably people respond to them. I'm also finding that the more vulnerable I allow myself to be in all my relationships, the more trust and intimacy I build.

I'll conclude with the armor piercing words of C. S. Lewis, from his book, *The Four Loves*: "To love at all is to be vulnerable. Love anything, and your heart will certainly be wrung and possibly be broken. If you want to make sure of keeping it intact, you must give your heart to no one, not even to an animal. Wrap it carefully round with hobbies and little luxuries; avoid all entanglements; lock it up safe in the casket or coffin of your selfishness."

Ouch! I think I'd rather risk exposing my throat. Sure, I stand a chance of getting bitten, but I might also end up being smitten. (Corny – I know - but that's me!)

Question for discussion or continued thought:

How can you be more vulnerable in your business relationships?

Robert Evans Wilson, Jr.

Be True to Yourself

Trying to impress the wrong people has a high price

One afternoon, back in 8th grade, I was hanging out with my pal Charlie, when I noticed copies of *Sports Illustrated* and *Car & Driver* magazines on his desk.

"Hey, I didn't know you were into cars and sports," I said.

"I'm not," he replied.

"But these magazines are addressed to you."

"I read them, because that's what the guys at school are talking about, and I want to join in. I want them to like me."

"Why don't you talk about what you like?"

Charlie just shrugged.

I couldn't believe Charlie would waste his time doing something he didn't like or care about, but a year later I was guilty of the same thing - only worse.

I was looking wistfully at pictures of cute girls in my high school yearbook when I said to my friend Tony, "I sure wish I knew how to talk to girls."

Tony replied, "The girls always talk to guys on the football team, you should go out for football."

It was all the motivation I needed. So, without ever having played the game before, without even knowing the rules, I joined the football team. I immediately found that I hated it. I had to run, in full pads, two or more miles every day in the hot sun. I had to lift weights, do sit ups and pushups, but the roughest part was tackling. I was six feet, two inches tall and weighed 150 pounds; I was a skinny bag of bones with no cushion and getting my body slammed to the ground really hurt. And, I was getting bruised for nothing; the girls still weren't talking to me.

I wanted to quit, but that would've meant losing face, so I stuck it out. Then one day, because of my height, I was asked to scrimmage on the defensive line with the Varsity team.

"Ten, twenty-two, seventeen, hut!" The quarterback yelled. I burst through the line and lunged forward to tackle him. I was inches from grabbing him, when suddenly I was hit so hard it lifted me in the air. I crashed to the ground face first, and when I tried to stand, I felt an explosion of pain that made me black out. Seconds later, I came to, but my leg would not move. When I looked down, it was bent in the wrong place, and I could see the bone pushing against my skin.

My decision to pursue a sport, not for the joy of it, but instead to impress someone that I did not even know put me in the hospital for two weeks. I had two surgeries, screws put into my bone, and a cast on my leg for six months. Adding insult to injury, walking on crutches didn't get the girls' attention either! It was a Lose/Lose situation.

You would think that I might have learned a lesson from that experience, but for years afterward, I repeated it again and again. I would pursue jobs, relationships, even leisure activities for the wrong reasons. In short, I was not true to myself. Sometimes when others are persuading us, we find ourselves doing things that make us feel uncomfortable. We ignore those feelings because we want to be accepted. Peer pressure doesn't end at age 18, it continues until we learn to listen to our feelings.

When we are motivated by something that makes us feel anxious, nervous or ill at ease, we need to pay attention to that feeling, and find its root. When we do, we will most likely find that we are uncomfortable because we are living a lie. I have learned that pursuing interests that bring me joy also give me confidence. My confidence then attracts people who want to be with me for who I am; and situations that generate greater satisfaction. I have finally found the formula for a Win/Win situation!

Question for discussion or continued thought:

Are you pursuing a goal that you are not interested in? How would you rather be spending your time?

Robert Evans Wilson, Jr.

Love Makes You Do Stupid Things

When you love yourself you attract respect

"I did not marry you to be married to a bartender!"

I should have paid more attention to the truth of her words; they clearly stated that she did not love me for who I am. In retrospect, it was the most obvious red flag she ever waved, but I was young, naive, and in love; and the real meaning went right over my head.

"I'm not a bartender; I'm a writer," I replied defensively.

"You're not a writer; you're not published."

It was a sucker punch! She knew I was writing eight hours a day, five days a week, and had for years. She knew I had completed dozens of short stories and two novels. She also knew... I had a stack of rejection letters to show for each.

My wife of three years was saying the same sort of things that my father had said. It was a sore spot for me, and a fight we would repeat many times.

A short time later, she asked me to become a partner in her business. She explained that she wanted to expand the business into several new states, and needed help to do it, but couldn't afford to hire someone. She said my experience in advertising would be beneficial to the company.

I was already feeling guilty that I was not more of a success in her eyes; and thinking I could win her love for good, I acquiesced. My decision meant working up to sixteen hours a day in an industry I hated. It meant traveling alone all over the southeastern United States by car, selling a product I didn't understand or believe in. Worst of all, it meant giving up writing full time. It was the biggest sacrifice I have made in my life. And, in the end, it went completely unappreciated.

Four years later a change in the industry caused us to close the business. By that time, I'd lost the momentum of writing fiction. On the other hand, I had learned so much from the experience of marketing my own company that I was able to take that knowledge and assist other companies in growing their business. But, the biggest benefit I gained from the experience wouldn't come until years later when we divorced.

Wisdom in the Weirdest Places

As our marriage deteriorated and the fighting escalated, one day she yelled at me, "You've never done anything for me."

"Are you kidding me?" I cried. "I gave up my biggest dream for you! I quit writing fiction to help you build your business, and I've never been able to get fully back into it."

She said, "That was a long time ago. I'm talking about now."

I was shocked; my loving gift had meant nothing to her.

Love is a powerful motivator that drives us to do all sorts of things. It puts a spring in our step, and at the beginning will even make us believe we live in a perfect world. Too often, however, we fail to begin the process in the right place.

The good news for me is that my divorce started me asking questions about myself. I needed to understand why my marriage didn't work. And, what my part had been in its demise. Surprisingly, I was eventually led to the wisdom of William Shakespeare, "To thine own self be true, and it must follow, as the night the day, thou canst not then be false to any man."

I learned that in order to win true love, that you must love yourself first. When you love yourself, that is, take care of your needs and dreams, you develop the self-confidence to attract a lover who will respect you. And, while there may be compromises, there will never be sacrifices.

Nowadays, when I find myself acting all goofy around an attractive woman, I start singing these words from rocker Big Bopper's *Chantilly Lace*:

Chantilly Lace had a pretty face;
And a pony tail hanging down.
That wiggle in the walk and giggle in the talk;
Makes the world go round.

There ain't nothing in the world like a big eyed girl;
That make me act so funny, make me spend my money;
Make me feel real loose like a long necked goose.
Oh baby that's what I like!

Then, I laugh myself back to reality.

Question for discussion or continued thought:

Are you taking care of your needs and dreams, or are you sacrificing them for someone else?

Wisdom in the Weirdest Places

Will Fame Buy Me Love?

What is it in your past that motivates you today?

I was polishing wine glasses behind the bar when the restaurant manager sat down across from me.

"Pour two shots of *Stoli*," he said.

I set up two pony glasses in front of him and poured the shots. He slid one back to me and said, "Cheers." It was a slow night and he wanted to chat.

"So, why do you write fiction?" He asked, knowing that was what I did all day before coming into work.

"Fame and fortune," I said, giving my standard answer.

"Not because you love it?"

"Oh, I love writing. I would do it even if I never got published, but making money from it is certainly a driving force."

"Any other reasons?" He inquired with a raised eyebrow.

"I suppose it's how I'll leave my mark on the world."

"Ah, your legacy."

"Yes. How about you, don't you want to do something that people will remember you for after you die?"

"So that strangers, people I don't know, will remember me?" He shook his head. "No. My legacy is my children."

"No kidding," I thought, "you have five of them."

He continued, "The time I spend with them, the experiences we have, the memories we make together will be enough for me."

I was 26 years old and his wisdom was beyond my comprehension. Nor did I understand what was actually driving me to write. Years later, I would learn that my ambition was deeply rooted in my early childhood experiences.

When you entered my childhood home, the large portrait in soft pastels that dominated the living room told you who ran things in my family. Everything in our household revolved around my mother: her interests, her needs, her goals.

My sister and I quickly learned that love came with a price tag: achievement. If we wanted love and attention we had to earn it. My sister became a straight-A student in school. She worried so much about achieving a perfect report card that she ended up in the hospital twice with bleeding stomach ulcers before she was even in high school. While I never reached the pinnacle my sister did, I felt the same pressure. I recall during my first year in school I would break down in tears whenever I couldn't answer a question or solve a problem on a test.

I grew up learning from my mother that love was conditional. Whether it was a blue ribbon for winning the hundred yard dash, or becoming an Eagle Scout, every scrap of approbation I received garnered a moment of precious loving attention and motivated me to strive for more. Sometime around second grade my mother praised me for a few lines of poetry I wrote, and the seed for becoming a writer was planted.

It wasn't until recently that I learned my mother was a narcissist, who was incapable of giving love. As a child, I didn't know that I could never be smart enough, attractive enough, accomplished enough - in short, good enough - to win the love I so desired.

As a young man in my twenties, I was determined to write a novel clever enough to become a best seller. Something that would win me the love I longed for. I wrote several, but none were quite good enough to be published. Years later, long after the passion for getting published wore off; I became a parent and discovered what my manager from the restaurant tried to tell me. Not having received it myself, I was determined as a parent to provide my children with a stable loving environment where they could flourish.

One of the ways I would do that was to make up bedtime stories for them. A story about a ghost kid became a favorite and they asked to hear it again and again. I kept adding to it, and they began to tell their friends about it. So many children wanted to hear it that I wrote *The Annoying Ghost Kid* down and published it. Ironically, my dream of creating a legacy with fiction may come from a story that evolved out of the legacy I am building with my children.

I sometimes wonder how many famous people are driven by the desire for an unattainable unconditional love they never received as children. Is there something from your distant past that still motivates you today?

Question for discussion or continued thought:

What are you doing to create your legacy?

Wisdom in the Weirdest Places

Who is the Puppet Master of Your Story?

Is your subconscious mind pulling the strings?

I discovered something interesting when I first started writing fiction. The more I developed a character, the more he would develop a mind of his own about what he would do or not do. Many times a direction I initially imagined the character would take was no longer possible based on the character's values. If I tried to force it, it would seem contrived, and, the reader would no longer find my character believable.

When that happens, I either have to rework my character or change the direction of my plot. If I don't, my reader will lose interest and put down the book. And, that is the last thing I want.

Later on in life, I was shocked to learn there was something else creating the motivation for my characters - my subconscious.

Sometimes a writer's stories are guided by his deepest unsatisfied needs. I'm not talking about the fact that most first novels are biographical and written from an author's own experience and knowledge. I'm talking about how his unresolved issues, ones that hark back to his childhood, will emerge as traits in his characters. What shocked me, when I recently revisited some of my earliest writings, was that I too had done this.

I first read about this in the book, *The Body Never Lies: The Lingering Effects of Hurtful Parenting* by psychotherapist Alice Miller. She writes of how the pain and suffering parents inflict on their children is retained in the psyche of the individual into adulthood. When the adult continues to repress the trauma he or she received, it causes illness.

She illustrates this point by comparing the lives and work of several famous writers. She notes that despite these writers' attempts to suppress their memories of being abused, the need to address their suffering and deal with it tended to emerge somewhere in their writing.

According to Miller, most people feel bound by the commandment to "Honor thy mother and father," despite how badly they were treated by their parents. Many of us, because of the love and caring we also received from our parents, suppress the memories of their mistreatment. Suppressing those memories causes stress to our bodies, and stress eventually causes illness.

According to David Eagleman, a neuroscientist, and author of *Incognito: The Secret Lives Of The Brain*, your brain does not like to keep things secret. He says your brain also does not like stress hormones. When you keep something secret, it increases the level of stress hormones in the body. The stress is created by the infighting between the part of your brain that wants to keep the secret, and the part that wants to reveal it. If you tell the secret - even by writing it in a private journal or sharing it in privileged conversation with a doctor or lawyer - it relieves its burden on your brain.

After reading those two books, I went back and re-read an unpublished novel I wrote in my twenties. I recognized that the traits I gave to the main character's father resembled those of my mother. As a child, I was alternately abused or engulfed by my mother.

As adults, my sister and I have joked that we never understood the proverb, *Don't cry over spilt milk* because as children we literally always cried over it because my mother would punish us severely for even accidentally spilling some on her clean floor. Subsequently, the father character in my book would beat his teenage son and scream at him for the mildest of infractions or accidents.

As a teenager, I found that I was enamored of my friend's mother. She was always gentle and calm. Even though she had five boisterous kids, she never lost her temper. I enjoyed hanging out at my friend's house instead of mine, because of the fear-free environment created by that woman. In my teenage opinion, she was the ideal mother. The one I wished I had. My mother's name was Barbara, so I would refer to my friend's mom as the Anti-Barbara.

In my novel, an abused teenager found a replacement father-figure in a boy three years older than himself who never bullied him and always treated him with respect. When I re-read my book, I recognized my friend's mom.

After my divorce, I went into therapy to understand the roots of my depression which seemed to go beyond losing my spouse. I learned that many of my issues were fallout from the abuse I suffered as a child. With that knowledge, I believe I can now go back to that novel I wrote so many years ago and rework the traits of my characters to make them more believable.

In revisiting my early work, I realized that in writing it, I was motivated by unresolved issues in my past. I was unconsciously expressing the effect my childhood trauma had on my life. What unresolved issues are unconsciously motivating your actions and directing your life?

Question for discussion or continued thought:

Do you see any patterns in your behavior that may stem from a childhood experience? If you can't see any patterns, ask a close friend to point them out.

CHAPTER SIX – POWER AND LEADERSHIP

In this chapter, I gain wisdom from dealing with the neighborhood bully, following a money trail, and by examining the leadership of some famous historical figures.

Are you a leader? Do you want to be a leader, or perhaps a better one? I'll share how you can learn to become a more effective leader. We will look at the difference between leaders and tyrants. We'll compare leadership and power. We will investigate the difference between earned and unearned power, as well as, power's connection to fear.

Bullies don't go away with childhood; and if you don't learn how to deal with them, they will continue to harass you throughout your life. As a child, I was a bully magnet; it was as if I had a permanent *Kick Me* sign taped to my back. I will share how my bully troubles continued until I learned how to stop giving them power.

Then we will look at how bullies push your buttons and how you are in control of their power. We will dissect the bully and see what his motivation for power over other people is all about. And, we will examine how we inadvertently encourage bullies.

You will read about money's relationship to power and how you can trace its influence. Plus, we'll consider the concept of honor and whether it has a place in today's world. Finally, you will learn about the best method for leading others.

Robert Evans Wilson, Jr.

Leadership vs. Power

Are you driven by goals or by power over others?

King George III asked Benjamin West, his American painter, what George Washington would do if he prevailed in the Revolutionary War. West replied, "He will return to his farm." The British monarch incredulously said, "If he does that, he will be the greatest man in the world." On December 23, 1783 Washington did just that and retired to Mount Vernon – despite the encouragement of many to stay in power. Despite the willingness of Americans to crown him king. Thirteen years later, he would do it once again.

In 1787, Washington was coaxed back to Philadelphia to attend the Constitutional Convention. While there he provided the leadership necessary to get the fractious delegates to settle down and complete the work of designing a new constitution. Afterwards, in 1789, he was elected the first President of the United States. He reluctantly ran for a second term in 1792. He refused to run for a third term, setting a precedent that lasted 150 years, and retired once again to his farm.

Abraham Lincoln said, "If you want to test a man's character – give him power." George Washington passed that test. Twice in his life he walked away from power and proved that he was indeed the greatest man in the world. He demonstrated that leadership is something that you give – not take – and that power should be used responsibly.

Washington died in 1799, the year that Napoleon Bonaparte became the ruler of France. In contrast to Washington, Napoleon could not acquire enough power. His legendary lust for command drove him to take over much of Europe. "Power is my mistress," he once claimed, "I have worked too hard at her conquest to allow anyone to take her away from me."

Years later, having lost all power and living in exile, he lamented "They wanted me to be another Washington."

History is rife with stories of people who abused their power. Abuse of power, however, is not just reserved for politicians and tyrants. It can be abused by managers, spouses, parents, peers and the list goes on. It is the lure of dominance over others, when it motivates people toward leadership roles, that is revealing. It reveals uncertainty, lack of confidence and fear.

It is said that power corrupts, but more often than not, it is a corrupted individual who is attracted to power. It is a feeling of inferiority, sometimes called a Napoleon Complex, that drives someone to control other people and to micro-manage their surroundings. Today we call such a person a Control Freak. Science fiction author, Robert Heinlein noted, "Anyone who wants to be a politician shouldn't be allowed to be one."

When we look at Abraham Maslow's *Hierarchy of Human Motivation* (Survival, Safety, Social, Esteem, Fulfillment), we see that someone who hungers for power is stuck in the second to bottom level which is Safety. A true leader has self-esteem and self-confidence and does not seek power to bolster his or her feeling of self worth. Thomas Jefferson observed that, "An honest man can feel no pleasure in the exercise of power over his fellow citizens."

A true leader is motivated by a goal. A goal common to his group whether that group is a company or a country. If you find yourself attracted to leadership, stop and check your motivation. Are you driven to share your gift of understanding in the endeavor of achieving a goal, or are you motivated by perquisites of position and the power you have over others? As John Quincy Adams said, "If your actions inspire others to dream more, learn more, do more and become more, you are a leader."

Question for discussion or continued thought:

What do you like best about your leadership role? How can you be a better leader?

Keep Your Power

*Giving your power to bullies robs you
of confidence and motivation*

"Baby Bobby! Baby Bobby!" The words stung and Mike knew it - he could read it in my face.

"Sticks and stones may break my bones, but names will never hurt me!" I yelled back.

Mike just laughed; he knew I didn't believe it. Bolstered by figuring out how to push my buttons, he continued to torment me as I walked home from school.

"Baby Bobby! Baby Bobby!"

The charge had an element of truth because I had cried several times in first grade, but I was now in fifth grade and had long outgrown my fear of school. I recalled the menacing teacher who pounded her paddle on our desks and threatened to spank us if we kept talking in class. She made several kids cry, but I was the one who got the reputation. It wasn't fair, but four years later I was still ashamed of my crying and Mike knew it. He continued the harassment.

"Baby Bobby! Baby Bobby!"

"Those are fighting words," I threatened.

He stuck his face right in mine and stated deliberately, "Baby... Bobby!"

I punched him in the nose, and suddenly he was the one crying. I had to fight several more boys that year before the name-calling stopped. It was not the solution I wanted, but it worked. It took me years to learn that the problem was mine; that I was giving away my power every time I reacted to taunting and teasing. And, it's a problem that doesn't go away with childhood.

Insecure adults wanting to feel superior will seek out your weaknesses and attempt to make you feel bad. Several years ago, I was invited to give my speech *The Innovator's Toolbox: Creative Thinking in Business* to a civic club luncheon. During the meal, a man at my table sneered, "Sooo, you're a motivational speaker. Well, motivate me!" His tone of voice said it all - the only difference between him and a school yard bully was the accompanying, "Na Na Na Na Nah."

I was shocked by the un-professionalism and thought, "I'm getting heckled, and I'm not even on stage yet." So, I laughed and said, "Dude, nobody can motivate you, but you."

He shocked me a second time by apologizing after my presentation. He explained that the club had a new speaker each week who tried to sell something, and that most of them were boring. To his surprise, he said he found my presentation entertaining and inspiring.

If we give in to bullies, they can rob us of our confidence and our motivation. Lately, I've worked with my children on how to not give their power away when kids assault them verbally. "Laugh it off," I tell them, "even if the words hurt. Fake it if you have to; the trick is to fool them into thinking it doesn't bother you."

Greek philosopher Epictetus may have said it best 2000 years ago, "Any person capable of angering you becomes your master; he can anger you only when you permit yourself to be disturbed by him."

My friend Rob Maxwell uses what he calls *Verbal Judo* to fend off words that hit like a fist. "In some martial arts," he explains, "you don't meet force with force. Instead, you take your opponent's thrust and redirect it away from you. Often their own energy works against them."

As an example, he told me of a college friend who was teasing him about losing his hair. Rob replied, "It's true John, I am losing my hair, but you were always the handsome one."

Question for discussion or continued thought:

What was your experience with bullies as a child? What has been your experience as an adult?

Robert Evans Wilson, Jr.

Fear vs. Power

*There is a correlation between fear and
the amount of power people seek*

 In 1971, George Johnson, a New York City policeman, arrested a man who was in a Times Square office building rifling through coats looking for money. Rather than call a paddy wagon, Johnson walked the man ten blocks across town to his precinct. The suspect accompanied him peacefully. As they walked, they smoked cigarettes and talked amiably. When they arrived at the station, Johnson learned that his arrestee was a wanted criminal with a history of attacking police officers. When asked by fellow officers how he managed to get the man there, he attributed the perp's placidity to having been treated with respect. I can't imagine that happening with many police officers today.
 America's police departments are increasing in size and becoming militarized, which is ironic because crime has been on a 20 year decline. America's police are also becoming more aggressive and bully-like. They are wearing paramilitary garb and gear. They are kicking down doors at the wrong houses, shooting innocent dogs, and routinely beating suspects with enough force to make those who beat Rodney King look like the Dalai Lama. The small town of Doraville, Georgia, a suburb of Atlanta, once celebrated in song as "a touch of country in the city" has even gone so far as to purchase a military tank for its SWAT team.
 According to CopBlock.org "From April 2009 to June 2010: 5,986 reports of [police] misconduct have been recorded; 382 fatalities were linked to misconduct; and $347,455,000 has been spent in related settlements and judgments."
 All of this police brutality is a symptom of a greater problem. My concern is with those who aspire to jobs with built-in power and prestige. I am concerned because I believe that the more power an office holds, the more ruthless - that is lacking in empathy - are the people who are attracted to it. I'm only referring to government jobs and political offices because those positions hold a monopoly on legal force. I am concerned about what may be the motivation behind the desire to hold these jobs.

Wisdom in the Weirdest Places

I have been a student of motivation for more than three decades, and I can think of thousands of motivations that tempt us daily: love, hunger, sex, comfort, health, status, and so on. However, the top motivator is fear. It is such a strong driver of our behavior that it may also form the basis for every other motivator in our lives. Fear is a prime motivator because it is rooted in our childhood experiences, and it moves us subconsciously.

David Richo, author of *When Love Meets Fear*, states, "When we notice a connection between our present fears and their origins in early life, we are finding out how much of our identity is designed by fear."

I believe there is a correlation between fear and the amount of power people seek. An individual's motivation for power is to acquire control over his environment. A certain amount of controlling behavior is a healthy natural survival instinct, but after a point it becomes harmful. When that happens normal survival is no longer the motivator. Underlying the quest for power is fear, and the desire for power is to eliminate fear. The more fearful a person is the more control over their environment they believe they need to feel safe. When they seek out public office this becomes a problem, because those who use power to assuage their own fear, also use fear against others to bolster and maintain their power. Citizens, who are also fearful, support the power-monger to the detriment of all.

The more controlling a business or a government becomes, the more it stifles creativity, innovation, and its ability to adapt to change. I am reminded of my college fencing instructor teaching me how to hold my foil, he said, "Hold it like you would hold a bird, tight enough that it can't get away, but not so tight that you kill it.

Merriam-Webster offers this definition of Power: "possession of control, authority, or influence over others." The average person understands that it must be earned. Known as "Referent Power," it is the ability of an individual to attract followers and build loyalty through charisma, leadership, and management skills. This power, and the prestige that goes with it, is only as good as the individual's honor and reputation allow.

In contrast, "Legitimate Power" or "Positional Power" is formal authority delegated to the holder of the office or position. This is the type of power managers have within a business enterprise; and it is the type of power granted to an agent of the government.

Subordinates and citizens must obey the office holders regardless of whether the power is earned or not.

Power itself is not evil; like money, it is indifferent and unbiased in its usefulness to the person who possesses it. It does not make the possessor evil; it is the possessor who uses it in evil ways.

In her book, *Freedom from Fear*, Nobel Peace Prize winner and Burmese opposition leader, Aung San Suu Kyi said, "It is not power that corrupts but fear. Fear of losing power corrupts those who wield it and fear of the scourge of power corrupts those who are subject to it."

Political and social power is the ultimate form of control. German philosopher, Friedrich Nietzsche, considered the domination of other humans as the exercising of control over one's environment. Michael Crichton, in his book *State of Fear*, said, "Social control is best managed through fear."

Joseph Stalin, Adolf Hitler, and Saddam Hussein were all raised by brutal parents who frequently beat them. They grew up living in daily fear. All of them went on to become dictators, who maintained complete control over their people through the use of extreme fear-producing violence.

The drive for safety through the War on Drugs and the War on Terror is turning the United States into a police state. The founders of the U.S. had experienced the abuse of power and worked to institutionally destroy power by reducing it to a minimum. They did this so that people would be free to pursue their happiness. Unfortunately, over the years, that freedom has been chipped away by people who are motivated by power.

I'm not saying that all agents of government are attracted to power, or that they were abused by their parents. Some, however, may have grown up feeling alienated or inadequate. They may not have been part of the in-crowd at school, or they may have been bullied or ostracized. Fast forward to today, and having the power of their office makes them feel secure.

People who have no legitimate or earned power and live in fear may resort to drugs and alcohol to numb it. Others' extreme fear have led them to violence in a last ditch effort to achieve a sense of power.

Everyone wants to be free of fear. It is prosperity, however, that is most likely to make people feel secure. Simply having the opportunity to achieve success makes people less fearful. Political and social freedom offer people a safe place to create their own fortune. Even if they are unsuccessful, most appreciate having had the unfettered opportunity, and take responsibility for the effort they made.

Rose Wilder Lane, daughter of *Little House on the Prairie* author, Laura Ingalls Wilder, was a world traveler who observed many oppressive governments. In contrast, she said, "An American could look at the whole world around him and take what he wanted from it, if he were able. Only criminal law and his own character, abilities and luck restrained him."

I would like to see an America that once again offers freedom of opportunity, so that our national fear and the growing police state can be abated. Let's return to the era when *Andy of Mayberry* represented America's police!

Question for discussion or continued thought:

How much control over your environment do you need to feel comfortable?

Robert Evans Wilson, Jr.

We Empower Bullies with Our Admiration

You love bullies... when they are on your side

Bullying has been in the news a lot lately. Awareness of the problem has spawned a number of programs designed to combat it. While I applaud this effort, I don't see bullying going away any time soon. The truth of the matter is that WE LOVE BULLIES. We reward and encourage them. We celebrate and cheer them on.

Watch any sitcom on TV, and we revel in the bullying. I enjoy watching the popular show, *How I Met Your Mother*, but in nearly every episode the so-called friends bully each other as well as other characters. And, like them, many of us bully our friends and family with collegial insults and practical jokes.

Of course, we tell ourselves, it is all in fun, and nothing is meant by it (or is it?), but the problem is that through our actions (and those of the characters on TV), we (and they) become role models for our children. They mimic us at school and on the playground. Your children may not be actively bullying someone, but they are laughing at those being bullied, and subsequently supporting, promoting, and fostering the continuation of bullying in our society.

We also admire bully-heroes in the movies: *Dirty Harry*, *The Godfather*, Captain Kirk of *Star Trek*, Gunnery Sergeant Hartman in *Full Metal Jacket*, Jules Winnfield in *Pulp Fiction*, Dr. Buddy Rydell in *Anger Management*, and so on. We love talk-show hosts like Bill O'Reilly and Neal Boortz when they bully guests and callers with whom we disagree.

Bullying doesn't stop with childhood, it only gets worse. Those who are successful bullies as children grow up to be bully-bosses or power-hungry politicians. They seek out and acquire power. We, in turn, admire and respect that power - that is as long as it is being used against our enemies, supports one of our causes, or we can convince ourselves that some good is coming from it. We only complain about it when that bullying power is used against us. Until we understand that power seekers are the most desperate people on the planet (see my article: Fear vs. Power) the problem will persist.

While I believe that Anti-Bullying programs are good, as a society we are talking out of two sides of our mouths. Because of that, I don't believe that bullying is going to go away. Most anti-bullying programs ask kids not to bully, not to be a consenting bystander, and to tell on bullies when they witness an attack. These are not realistic expectations in a society where most people fear the recrimination of their peers.

These programs also teach children to avoid bullies at all costs, which doesn't really serve the victim in the long run. A better solution is to teach children how to develop self-esteem and self-confidence. When we teach kids how to believe in themselves, we give them the fundamental tools they need to stand up to bullies.

In my children's novel, *The Annoying Ghost Kid*, Duke, the ghost, is the ultimate bully because, with his power of invisibility, he can attack his victims right in front of the teacher with impunity. Even worse his victims get blamed for his pranks. For Corky and Jill, the victims, they have no one to turn to, and there is no recourse but to learn how to stand up to the bully on their own. Duke has super powers which means they can't simply hit back; they must learn how to outwit him.

I am frequently invited to make *Author Visits* to elementary schools. I explain to the children the weaknesses of bullies (in brief, that they lack self-esteem and seek approval through their bullying), so that potential victims know they have power over the bully.

I then give them two simple techniques to use in the event of an attack (one for verbal attacks and one for physical attacks). Both are easy to remember, so that a child, caught unaware by a bully attack, is less likely to panic and show fear.

In brief, those are as follows: for a verbal attack, I teach them to agree with the bully's taunt, laugh, then walk away. For a physical attack, I teach them to thrust out their hand, palm up, like a traffic cop indicating, "STOP," and yell, "BACK OFF!" all the while holding eye-contact with the bully and giving him/her what I call their "serious face."

In life, we must all learn to deal with bullies on our own because they do not go away with adulthood. In fact, they get worse. The sooner a person learns how to deal with bullies the better, and the easiest time to do that is when they are young.

Question for discussion or continued thought:

What are some of the ways that you see tacit approval of bullying?

Empathy for Bullies

Finding the motivation that drives bullies to attack

I was sitting on the bench in the locker room dressing out for P. E., when a big kid I hadn't met before sat down next to me. With a broad smile on his face he said, "Hey."

Appreciating a potential new friend, I smiled back and replied, "Hi."

He then he shoved me off the bench, slammed my locker shut, and started laughing. The kids around us laughed too.

I got up off the floor and yelled, "Not funny!" then tried to sit back down on the bench. Once again he shoved me off. When I tried again, he hit me hard on my shoulder.

Reeling in pain, I stood and waited until he finished dressing before I could get back into my locker. I was thirteen years old. It was my first year in high school. Jerry, the big kid, was fifteen years old. Apparently he'd been held back a couple of grades.

The next day the same thing happened, and again the day after. On the following day, I tried avoiding the problem by arriving early, but with only five minutes between classes that proved to be impossible.

I tried distracting him with friendly conversation, "Hey Jerry, did you see *Alias Smith and Jones* on TV last night?"

"Yeah, it was good." Then he body slammed me off the bench. Again the kids around us laughed. And, again I was forced to stand and wait until he was finished.

The problem continued for three weeks, and on a few occasions I was scolded by the coach for being tardy to the gym. I couldn't tell him why I was late because Jerry had the mirth of our fellow classmates and I feared their ostracizing more than Jerry's fist.

My few friends in the class kept asking me what I was going to do about the problem. The rest of the kids just looked at me with contempt. It made me feel isolated and totally not "cool" for being unable to find a solution.

Finally in frustration I went to my dad.

"How do you feel about my getting suspended from school?" I asked him.

"What!" he cried.

Wisdom in the Weirdest Places

I then explained the situation, and how I felt the only solution was to stand up to Jerry and fight him. To my surprise, he agreed.

"Son, I understand that you have to fight this boy. If you get suspended, you will do so with my good graces."

That was an awesome bonding moment with my father; and even though I was afraid of Jerry and knew that I was probably going to get hurt, it fortified my resolve to stand up to him.

The next day, with butterflies in my stomach, I arrived as early as I could and took my seat on the bench. As expected Jerry shoved me off the bench and slammed my locker shut. To his surprise, I got off the floor and started punching him as fast and hard as I could.

On his face, I saw the shock that he never expected me to retaliate, but that didn't last long. Jerry was taller and much more muscular than me. He simply picked me up and threw me against the lockers and laughed. The pain shooting through my back mirrored the explosive sound of my body hitting the metal doors. From the ground, I could see him looking around the room for approval, smiling and nodding at those who laughed with him.

In that instant, when he wasn't paying attention, I scrambled off the floor and started hitting him again. I landed one good punch on his jaw. He was no longer laughing, but he still seemed completely unfazed by my fists. Once again, he picked me up and threw me into the lockers. As I hit the floor, he ordered me to stay down.

Ignoring him, I leapt to my feet.

"Fight! Fight!" someone yelled, and 60 boys who were dressing, stopped and rushed over to watch.

Suddenly, Jerry and I found ourselves in the middle of a space no more than four feet wide surrounded by boys cheering for one or the other of us. We both had our fists up and were circling around wondering who was going to make the next punch, when someone yelled, "Coaches are coming!"

Everyone in the room dispersed instantly. Jerry and I, panting from the adrenaline and exertion, sat down side by side and opened our lockers.

Three coaches walked through the room demanding, "Who's fighting?" "Somebody tell us who was fighting!"

No one said a word. Everyone silently finished dressing. The coaches finally left but not without warning us that fighting was not allowed.

I didn't get suspended, and Jerry never bothered me again.

In my article, *Keep Your Power* (see Chapter Six), I wrote that bullying is not just a childhood phenomenon. We must learn to get over our fear of the consequences of standing up for ourselves because bullies never go away.

One of the problems is, that as a society, we don't really look at the motives behind bullying. Bullying is a trickle down phenomenon, which is most likely learned at home. Most bullies are bullied by someone else somewhere. Many of us know that bullies are insecure. They don't feel important, loved, or cared for. Bullies seek attention, so that they will feel wanted, desired, and appreciated. Unfortunately, they don't know how to achieve that through normal channels.

If we can take a moment to have empathy for them, perhaps we can give them what they need, and cut off the problem at the source. Today, I can look back and see that Jerry probably felt inadequate because he was nearly two years older than everyone in his class. I never saw him again after that year. He turned 16 over the summer, and I heard he dropped out of school which probably added to his sense of unimportance. As an eighth-grader, all I could see was the violence. I didn't have the maturity or the self-confidence to reach out to him as a friend. In hindsight, I wish I did.

Question for discussion or continued thought:

What are some ways that we can show empathy for bullies and help them acquire the self-esteem necessary to function positively in society?

Wisdom in the Weirdest Places

The Buck Starts Here

Looking for motive? Follow the money trail

Recently I participated in a *Murder Mystery* weekend at a bed and breakfast lodge. Every guest was a given a role to play. There were eight suspects; each of whom had one or more of the following: *Means*, *Opportunity* and *Motive*. Having the means and opportunity was very important, but having the right motivation was the key to solving the puzzle. We interviewed the suspects, collected clues, then presented who we thought was the killer and why. It was great fun, but I failed to figure out *who done it*. I was very logical and surmised that a suspect with a monetary motive was the one. But, it turned out to be one with the emotional motive of anger and revenge.

Never-the-less, money is a powerful motivator. It is the original carrot dangling from the stick.

My friend Bill, the computer wizard, told me years ago, "I always follow the money." Meaning that he would learn those computer skills that paid the best. I did the same thing in my early years as a writer. I found journalism fun, but that advertising paid better. Subsequently, I pursued advertising work and honed my skills in motivating people to buy.

The exciting thing about money, or more specifically: prosperity, is that it is a great equalizer. Prosperity has a way of eliminating envy, hatred and bigotry. Increased wealth makes people more tolerant and giving. The formula for prosperity is simple: economic freedom plus property rights. In other words, minimal regulation and the right to keep what you earn.

Clearly we all know that money is a reliable method for motivating people. But, if you ever want to discover the motivation behind an action that appears to be random, backtracking the money trail is frequently a good way to find it. For example, have you ever noticed one of your favorite products disappearing from the store where you buy it? It probably means that there were not enough customers for it and the store quit carrying it. If, however, you can't find it anywhere, then the lack of users is widespread and the manufacturer discontinued it.

Sometimes, however, the money trail is even longer, and more convoluted. You've heard it said many times that *Money is Power*.

It's true especially in politics. Money has the power to persuade people (some might prefer to say *buy* them); and as such it has the power to distort markets and even economies.

I recall a hot summer day, back in the late 1980s, when, after mowing the lawn, I popped open an ice cold soda pop and drained it in one long gulp. Moments later I was on the floor with a painful spasm in my back. It lasted nearly half an hour, and when it was over I made an appointment with my doctor. It turned out that I was allergic to the corn syrup in the soda.

"How could that be?" I asked. I'd drank thousands of sodas without having that reaction. What I learned was that up until that particular can of soda all the ones I'd drank before were made with sugar. So, I asked, "Why would they switch to corn syrup?" The answer was that the cost of sugar had gone up; and they did not want to raise the price. "Why was sugar more expensive?" Because Congress placed a tariff on imported sugar. "Why did Congress do that?" Sugar growers in Florida asked them to because they did not want to compete with low-cost Caribbean sugar. "Why would Congress comply when it would raise prices on all products made with sugar; and cause manufacturers to move to other countries leaving thousands of workers unemployed?" Because the sugar growers donated lots of campaign money to a majority of the members of Congress. The trail ends, and the puzzle is solved.

It turns out that my favorite soda pop is still made with sugar in every country on the planet except the United States. One day, I'm going to get a craving and drive a thousand miles to Mexico. Talk about motivation!

Question for discussion or continued thought:

How has money motivated you? How can you use money to motivate others?

Wisdom in the Weirdest Places

On my Honor

*Is the concept of honor simply
too difficult to understand?*

With the morning mist still on the Hudson River, and the sun just kissing the cliff tops of the New Jersey Palisade, Aaron Burr, Vice President of the United States shot and killed former Secretary of the Treasury, Alexander Hamilton. Political opponents for years, the duelists faced each other after Burr sent these words to Hamilton: "Political opposition can never absolve gentlemen from the necessity of a rigid adherence to the laws of honor."

Once upon a time people were motivated by honor. Acquiring it, maintaining it, defending it. Bitter duels were fought in its name. I don't hear much talk about honor anymore.

Could it be the concept of honor is too difficult to understand? Is it truly ineffable - impossible to define - to the point that no one really knows what it means? As a virtue, it has certainly taken a beating when some cultures identify the murder of family members as an "honor killing," and when criminals such as the Mafia call themselves "men of honor."

I looked it up in the *Webster Dictionary* and found the words "reputation" and "integrity." But, honor seems to be more than that. It is similar to the definition of character which is: "what you do when no one is watching." Again, it must be more than that. So, I researched what some historical figures said about it. Most of them described honor by what it is not.

Thomas Jefferson said, "Nobody can acquire honor by doing what is wrong." OK, we'll assume he means you must do what is right or good. The problem may be that by today's standards those are up for debate.

The ancient Greek playwright, Sophocles, also tells us what not to do, but at the same time defines what is wrong: "Rather fail with honor than succeed by fraud."

Which reminds me of my favorite quote from *The Kite Runner* by Khaled Hosseini: "There is only one sin, only one. And that is theft. Every other sin is a variation of theft....When you kill a man, you steal a life. You steal his wife's right to a husband, rob his children of a father. When you tell a lie, you steal someone's right to the truth. When you cheat, you steal the right to fairness."

Of course fraud is theft, and any way in which someone defrauds another is wrong. Today, however, I feel as if fraud is the new coin of the realm. That it has become an accepted part of our culture. I hear so many conflicting claims from government officials - whether it is about global warming or the cause of terrorism or how to repair the economy - that sometimes I don't really know what to believe. It reminds me of a bit of graffiti I saw years ago: *Believe nothing of which you hear and only half of what you see.*

I also like this observation by former U.S. President, Herbert Hoover, "When there is a lack of honor in government, the morals of the whole people are poisoned." In other words, if we feel like our government is cheating us, then a kind of a trickle-down corruption starts to exist. Now that is frightening indeed.

Others say that honor is something that we are born with, and that we must strive to keep it. German philosopher, Arthur Schopenhauer, said, "Honor has not to be won; it must only not be lost." Here is a similar statement by French author and poet, Nicholas Boileau, "Honor is like an island, rugged and without shores; once we have left it, we can never return." Still, neither tells what it is.

And, you can't really claim to have it, as Ralph Waldo Emerson notes, "The louder he talked of his honor, the faster we counted our spoons." Could it be something that only other people can observe in you?

Leonardo da Vinci, endeavored to define it as, "He who sows virtue reaps honor." One of the best definitions I found is from journalist, Walter Lippmann, "He has honor if he holds himself to an ideal of conduct though it is inconvenient, unprofitable, or dangerous to do so."

I recall my father teaching me about honor and duty, and I have endeavored to teach my sons about it as well. I hope they will grow up in a world where honor has a resurgence and people are motivated by it once again.

Question for discussion or continued thought:

What is your definition of honor? Can honor still be a motivator in today's world?

Robert Evans Wilson, Jr.

Example is Everything

Whether you intend to or not, you lead by example

As you finish reloading your rifle, you realize there's a lull in the fighting. There is no gunfire; no explosions; the screaming and yelling have subsided. After three hours of battle, it's become relatively quiet on both ships. You take a moment to assess the situation.

From the beginning you've been at a disadvantage. The enemy's ship is newer, bigger, faster, and has more guns than yours. You admit she's a beauty, built to be a warship, unlike yours which was retrofitted for war from an aging merchant ship designed for trade and cargo.

Your opponent hit you pretty hard with its first volley. Those big guns ripped huge holes in the sides of your ship. You had some pretty big guns too, but the first one fired exploded and took out all the cannon around it. Now that deck is useless and most of the men on it are dead.

The battle started at nightfall, and you've been fighting by moonlight. There are other ships on both sides, but in the smoke and the darkness no one can tell friend from foe. One of your own ships, thinking you were the enemy, fired a broadside which killed a dozen of your men.

You believe you have the smarter captain. He has outmaneuvered the enemy at least once. He saw that the big warship had turned in such a way as to lose all the wind in its sails. Rather than take the opportunity to flee, he took the more daring option of sailing right up against it, so that the two ships were side by side. Your captain was even the first to start lashing your ship to the enemy's so they could not get away.

At that point the battle really became fierce. The enemy's cannons continued to blow holes in your ship. However, now with the two ships locked together, the cannon balls shoot straight through the hull and out the existing holes on the other side limiting the destruction.

Unfortunately, the damage has been done, water is pouring in and your ship is sinking. You can feel it and see it. Your top deck is already lower than the enemy's. Half an hour ago, they tried to take

Wisdom in the Weirdest Places

advantage of that by boarding your ship. You and your fellow sailors engaged in savage hand-to-hand combat led by your captain until you forced the enemy to retreat back to their ship.

Nevertheless, things are looking pretty grim. You're not just sinking; one of the decks below is on fire. Plus, all your sails are aflame, lighting up the night and making all the damage to your ship clearly visible. You can see that half your crew is dead. You were outnumbered to begin with, now the odds seem impossible. You can feel the fatigue starting to seep into your muscles, and you figure the fight is over and that you'll soon be in chains in the warship's brig.

The British Captain is thinking the same thing, and yells across the bow, "Do you surrender?"

You look around, but the captain is nowhere in sight. A shipmate says the captain and the first mate are dead. Suddenly, the ship's carpenter takes it upon himself to give up and starts yelling, "We must strike the colors!" You think the ship must be gravely damaged and sinking faster than you thought if the ship's carpenter is crying out for surrender.

You hear someone shout, "Stop!" It's the captain, who has just appeared out of the smoke. The carpenter doesn't hear and continues running toward the flag pole. The captain pulls a pistol from his belt. You think he is going to shoot the carpenter, but instead he throws it with pinpoint accuracy hitting the man in the head and knocking him out cold.

Once again, the British captain cries out, "Do you surrender?"

Your captain, John Paul Jones, replies loud enough for everyone on both ships to hear, "I have not yet begun to fight!"

A rallying cheer erupts on board your ship, and you think, "This man is amazing!" You fire your musket as everyone on board begins to fight again. You double your efforts and reload faster than you ever have before. A shipmate throws a grenade, hitting a pile of munitions on the British ship. There is a massive explosion and moments later, you and your crew swarm over the gunwales onto the top deck of the enemy ship. Within minutes that deck is captured and the British captain surrenders by pulling down his flag.

You look at Captain Jones and think, "It looks like we had the advantage all along."

Time and again, John Paul Jones led by example and motivated his crew to fight on against unimaginable odds. That hard won naval victory is, to this day, considered the most important in U.S. history because it set the standard for the American navy.

Leading successfully begins with being a good role model. I recall my parents saying, "Do as I say, not as I do." In the end, I always did as they did. What they did not realize is that whether you intend to or not, you always lead by example. Mahatma Gandhi understood this when he said, "We must become the change we want to see."

When you communicate by example, you say non-verbally that you would not ask your employees to perform anything that you are not willing to do yourself.

Or as Albert Schweitzer observed, "Example is not the main thing in influencing others. It is the only thing."

Question for discussion or continued thought:

How can you lead better by serving as an example?

CHAPTER SEVEN – MAKING BOLD COMMITMENTS

In this chapter, I found wisdom in volunteering when I really didn't want to, and by allowing myself to risk being embarrassed.

We will examine how being bold opens many doors of opportunity. Boldness is about being brave and daring; and it's about becoming confident and self-assured. When you take on these characteristics - even in baby steps - you will be rewarded in ways that you could not imagine before you started.

In the first article, I share with you an epiphany I had that came from taking a bold step more out of desperation than from desire.

Being bold doesn't mean you have to be audacious, because taking even a small step outside your comfort zone can be transformational. It is not about being cocky, but when you experience the success that follows a courageous move - you will feel like you're walking taller.

We will look at how making a commitment has an almost magical quality about it that seems to make the planets line up to help us achieve our goals.

Finally, we will look at how our pride, in conjunction with our fear of embarrassment, keeps us from taking those initial bold steps.

Robert Evans Wilson, Jr.

What's the Worst that can Happen?

Being bold has enormous rewards

"Who wants to give their oral report first?" asked Mrs. Davis, my sixth grade teacher.

The dreaded day had finally arrived when each of us would have to stand in front of the room and speak to the class. The butterflies in my stomach were flapping a tornado.

Not a single hand went up. In fact, there was no movement in the room at all. There wasn't a desk creaking under the shifting weight of a single body, no paper rustling, no pencils scratching, not even a cough. Nothing. The room had never been quieter. Every kid was sitting as still as a statue. The anxiety in the classroom was palpable.

"If someone doesn't volunteer, then I will start picking you at random."

Every student suddenly wished for invisibility. I saw a few heads bow in the hopes of achieving it. But, mostly I saw wide-eyed fright - the deer in the headlights look - predominate the room.

She started scanning the room and said, "Okay, then I'll choose..."

I couldn't take it anymore; I just wanted to get it over with. Almost involuntarily, my hand shot up. Then to my surprise, unexpected benefits started coming my way immediately.

Mrs. Davis began praising me for my courage. She said that I would set the standard by which everyone following me would be judged. Her praise gave me instant confidence, and I could feel the nervousness melt away. I stood before the class and delivered my report with authority and self-assurance. I then got to sit down and relax, and enjoy everyone else's presentation without the fear that I would called on next.

It was a seminal moment - a life changing experience - I discovered that being bold could have enormous rewards. It was a lesson I have carried ever since.

A few years would pass before I tested my boldness again. I was interested in student government in high school, and on several occasions ran for office. Each time, however, I chose to run for the lesser offices and each time I lost. My last opportunity to run came at the end of eleventh grade. This time I threw all caution to the wind and went after the big prize: President of the Student Council.

I won. As a result I enjoyed a full year of confidence building responsibility. The rewards I enjoyed for that moment of daring were enormous. I went from being just another kid in the school to being treated like an adult by the teachers and administration. It opened more opportunities than I could have imagined.

Tennis star, Billie Jean King, once said, "Be bold. If you're going to make an error, make a doozy, and don't be afraid to hit the ball."

I have also learned that when you go for the big prize, you will not face a lot of competition. I'm not saying the competition isn't tough - there just aren't as many competitors. That's true in business too. Go for the higher paying job. Pitch your product to the biggest client. Ask the most beautiful girl or handsome guy for a date.

Emily Dickinson said, "Fortune befriends the bold." So, the next time you have an opportunity to take a bold step, ask yourself this, "What's the worst that can happen?" Then go for it!

Question for discussion or continued thought:

Is there a bold step you can take today that would move you closer to your goals?

Robert Evans Wilson, Jr.

Take the Plunge

*Commit by jumping in feet first,
then watch where it takes you*

"I hate you! I'm going to kill you tonight after you fall asleep." screamed nine year old Jerry to his foster mother. It was hard to believe such hateful words could come from this adorable child with big blue eyes and an impish face.

Dee loves Jerry and wants to adopt him, but these angry outbursts frighten her (I have changed their names to protect their privacy). She tries to imagine what he will be like, if he does not learn how to control his anger, when he is a teenager and out sizes her in both height and weight. The court says she has to make a decision this month on whether or not to keep him. And, she is torn about what to do.

Two years ago, 45 year old Dee, a beautiful redhead who never married, decided that the only way she was going to have children would be to adopt. She became a foster parent with the hopes of finding a child she could love and raise. Within a couple of months, the agency called with an eight year old redheaded boy who resembled her enough to be her own. Dee was warned that Jerry had serious anger issues. The boy had been passed from foster home to foster home since birth and had never known a stable home life. Dee's heart went out to Jerry.

While she comes from a large family and is Auntie Dee to many, she had no firsthand experience raising children herself. Jumping into the deep end with a troubled little boy was the proverbial "sink or swim" situation, but Dee threw herself completely into it. She went from being a carefree single to a single Mom with a steep learning curve. It's one thing to start from scratch with a baby, where you get to learn as you go along; it's a whole other story when a child comes pre-programmed with years of neglect and abuse.

She went from just having to get up and go to work, to having to get up and get a little boy ready for school. There's homework to be checked, meals to be prepared, additional laundry, and all the shuttling to and from school, sports, and counseling. It's not all work, she is also enjoying the fun parts of raising a child: going to

Wisdom in the Weirdest Places

the playground, reading stories, cooking meals together, and savoring the adoring words of, "I love you, Mommy."

The deadline to adopt or not is only weeks away. With each passing day, Jerry becomes more belligerent. When Dee asks him to put on his shoes, or brush his teeth, he refuses, throws a fit, and calls her unprintable names.

Adding to this dilemma is that Dee was laid off from her job in April. Once she adopts, the resources that have been provided by the government will end. She has been able to pick up some temp work here and there, but she is concerned that she may not have the money necessary to provide Jerry with the ongoing counseling he needs.

Dee and I met at an advertising convention five years ago, and even though we live three thousand miles apart we have become good friends. I have followed her saga with Jerry closely. Recently, knowing that I'm a single parent, she asked me what I would do. Here's what I said, "I encourage you to adopt Jerry. I believe when he sees you make that commitment his behavior will improve. His behavior is getting worse right now because he is afraid. In his mind, it is safer for him to purposely fail than it is for him to get his expectations up that you will adopt him. He has been there before - over and over again - and has been disappointed. He knows how much it hurts; and it would cause him too much pain to give in to hope again - and lose. He has created a survival mechanism that is all about fighting you and threatening you because if you reject him, he will at least have reason he understands. Jerry is shielding his heart from being broken again."

"Dee, I know it's a risk, but I hope you'll choose him. I believe it will save his life. You have great resources already available to you through your family. And, in my experience when you commit to something, more resources always appear. I believe with all my heart that he will become the son you want - because you will have shown him that that is your intention and he will want to live up to it."

If you are sitting on the fence about a commitment, my suggestion is to go for it. Jump in feet first and find out where it takes you. I'll write more on commitment next time.

Note: Dee did decide to take the plunge, and has adopted Jerry.

Question for discussion or continued thought:

What is keeping you from making a commitment?

Wisdom in the Weirdest Places

The Magic of Commitment is no Mystery

*How opportunities arise that you
ordinarily would not notice*

"Who wants to be chairperson of the Fundraising Committee?" asked the President.

The room became very quiet, and as I glanced around the table, I saw a dozen perfect poker faces. No one wanted this responsibility. No one was going to commit.

After a moment the President continued, "This is our most important committee, without funding we cannot put on our program to teach leadership skills to high school students."

It was my first year on the executive committee of the Georgia chapter of the *Hugh O'Brian Youth Foundation* (HOBY). I had no idea how they had previously raised the $50,000 a year that was necessary to operate. As an advertising consultant, I'd helped raise millions of dollars for several national non-profits with direct mail advertising. So, I thought, "How hard can this be?"

I raised my hand and said, "I'll do it." A collective sigh issued from the group and several congratulated me on accepting such a big responsibility. I basked in the accolades and beamed an appreciative smile back to everyone.

It didn't take but a few days before I was lamenting, "What the heck was I thinking?"

I learned that my predecessors had solicited most of the money in a handful of big donations from a small group of donors. Unfortunately, those donors were feeling tapped out, and were no longer willing give. I couldn't back out of the job - I'd made a commitment! All I needed was a Plan B.

I quickly got on the phone and starting telling everyone I knew what I was trying to accomplish. Someone suggested that I apply for grants from the charitable foundations of large corporations. Three dozen applications later, I had nothing to show for my hours of work. I now needed a Plan C.

When I volunteered, I had a vague notion that I would simply raise all that money with a direct mail campaign. The campaigns I'd worked on I the past had mega-budgets in the hundreds of thousands of dollars and major advertising agencies involved. I had no budget and only five or six volunteers to help out. Even if I had a budget, I didn't know to whom I should send my direct mail solicitations. I knew from experience that retirees are among the best donors, but purchasing a list of generous givers was expensive!

About that time a fellow in the concession business who I worked with when I was president of my neighborhood association, called me to see if I knew any groups that could operate a beer stand at an annual weekend-long outdoor rock concert. I said, "Do I ever!"

We raised $10,000 in three days. We did such a good job, we were asked to come back every year. It was a big job that required more people than we had, so we recruited help from outside of the organization. That turned out to be easy because the people who volunteered got into the concert free for that day. Many of them had so much fun, they volunteered to help put on the youth leadership seminars for which HOBY is known. As an unexpected side benefit, it became our best vehicle for recruiting volunteers for the next several years.

I still had $40,000 to raise. I learned from one old-timer that in years past HOBY received donations from the Kiwanis clubs. I called a friend who was a member. He told me that HOBY was on the *Kiwanis International* approved list of charities. This was huge! It meant we already had a foot in the door. He then helped me acquire a mailing list of all the clubs in the state.

I now had what I needed for a direct mail campaign. I wrote to every club and asked them to sponsor one child from each high school in their area. I then set up a phone bank of volunteers to call the clubs and ask them directly for a donation. We raised more than we needed! Best of all, we now had two programs in place for raising funds year after year.

I have found over the years that when you commit to a project whether it is starting a business, a new relationship or learning a new skill, opportunities arise that you ordinarily would not have noticed.

William Hutchinson Murray, from his 1951 book entitled *The Scottish Himalayan Expedition* says it best, "Until one is committed, there is hesitancy, the chance to draw back. Concerning all acts of initiative (and creation), there is one elementary truth, the ignorance of which kills countless ideas and splendid plans: that the moment one definitely commits oneself, then Providence moves too. All sorts of things occur to help one that would never otherwise have occurred. A whole stream of events issues from the decision, raising in one's favor all manner of unforeseen incidents and meetings and material assistance, which no man could have dreamed would have come his way."

I've always called this *Initiating the Discovery Process* because when you combine your commitment - your powerful desire - to solve a problem or satisfy a particular need, your subconscious mind will work on it 24/7.

To understand how this works, think of the last time you were in the market for a new car. After shopping the market, you selected a particular make and model. Up until that time you hardly ever noticed that car on the road, but now that you have committed to it - suddenly you see them everywhere! Opportunities present themselves in the same way.

Commitment has a way of creating its own motivation. Go for it - and see what comes your way!

Question for discussion or continued thought:

Which of your goals would benefit from a fresh commitment?

Robert Evans Wilson, Jr.

It's Your Pride and Vanity, Stupid

Let yourself be embarrassed - it's worth it!

When I was a boy, I heard a story about a hot dog stand owner, who would put on a clown costume, then stand on the sidewalk everyday and wave motorists into his business. He was so successful; he was able to send his son to college. Upon graduating from college, the son, now worldly and sophisticated, was embarrassed by his father's antics. He convinced his dad that was not the way to get customers. The father, taking the advice from his college-educated son, retired his clown costume, and stopped waving drivers into his restaurant. Overtime business dropped off, and they went out of business.

Whether or not that story is true, I recall the ubiquitous TV commercials of a low-cost furniture store owner in Atlanta during the 1980s and 90s. He sported a flowing mane of hair and a thick beard, and called himself the Wolfman. It was an apt name, as he really looked the part. The ads were excruciatingly corny, but exceedingly memorable. Those advertisements were widely mocked, but he was able to put aside his pride and vanity, and continue making them. He made more than 500 of them, each of which were on-the-air thousands of times. They pulled flocks of people into his stores, and in turn he enjoyed a great deal of success.

Too often we allow our self-consciousness - our fear that people may judge us negatively - to keep us from taking risks or trying new things.

I love the scene, in the movie *Breaking Away,* when Dave Stoller stands outside the girls' dormitory and serenades, in a cracking voice, an Italian love song to Katherine, a girl he wants to date. At first her friends laugh, and she acts embarrassed, but he continues on and eventually she becomes flattered by his bold gesture and goes to him.

Occasionally I'm asked to coach people in public-speaking, most of whom want to get over their stage-fright. I begin by explaining to them, that their fear comes from being too focused on themselves and not on their words.

"You are thinking about yourself and not your message which is all the audience wants. You are worried about what you look like, how you sound, and whether or not you're going to make a mistake. This is *all about you*, when your speech should be *all about your audience*. Think of your speech as a gift you are giving them, and that your content speech is all that matters. If you focus your thoughts on making sure your audience receives the vital information they need and want, then you won't have time to think about yourself."

I learned this valuable lesson at a networking event years ago. I was talking with a woman I had just met. We had already exchanged businesses cards and described our companies to each other, when our hostess came over to greet us. She asked the woman if she had heard me speak. She replied, "No, Rob was just telling me he is a speaker, but I have never seen him."

The hostess then added, referring to an exercise I have the audience carry out in my innovation seminars, "Well, if you do, he will have you standing on your chair." Suddenly the woman gasped, and said, "Wait, I have seen you speak!" She then proceeded to tell where and when she had heard me, as well as, recounting one of my stories which illustrated one of the creative-thinking techniques I teach, and how she had used it in her business.

I stood there deeply humbled; she remembered a story I told, but she did not remember my face, my name or my company name. The purpose I had set out to achieve had been accomplished; she found my information useful and implemented it.

The lesson I learned was to keep telling good stories, but give the audience something with my name on it to take home, so they could remember and recommend me to others.

If you have a goal you wish to achieve, or an idea you want to try, don't let your fear of embarrassment keep you from it. Focus on the reward and take a bold step toward it.

Question for discussion or continued thought:

How have you let self-consciousness keep you from taking a risk? How can you promote a business, an idea, or a relationship with a potentially embarrassing activity?

CHAPTER EIGHT – BELIEVING IN YOURSELF

In this chapter, I gather wisdom from an ant, a copy cat, and coaching a losing Little League baseball team.

We'll look at how believing in yourself will bring you remarkable rewards. The techniques for developing self-belief are simple yet powerful; I'll show you how.

In the first article, we'll examine how a positive self-belief is acquired, and why it is the first ingredient in a recipe for success. Then we'll look deeper into the ways you can acquire that necessary belief in yourself.

We'll also look at methods you can use to engender that belief in others. Then we'll consider the dangers of criticism and how to safely use it - if you must. Better than criticism is the power of praise, and I'll share a personal story of how both have worked in my life.

Finally, we'll look at what makes us flinch or choke - that is fail - when we have all the talent, skill, and preparation to succeed.

Robert Evans Wilson, Jr.

The Main Ingredient

A recipe for success needs this secret

In 1907, during a major league baseball game, second base was stolen 13 times by the winning team. The catcher for the losing team, Branch Rickey, was unable to pick off even a single runner. That record stands to this day. It also spelled the end of Rickey's career as a baseball player after just two seasons. With nothing else to do, he went to college and law school.

Six years later, he returned to major league baseball. This time as a manager – and what a manager he turned out to be! He created the modern baseball farm system which enables major league teams to nurture and develop future stars through their minor league teams. He was the first to establish a permanent spring training facility in Florida. He changed the way statistical analysis is used in baseball by proving that *on-base percentage* is more important than *batting average*. Branch Rickey is best known, however, for breaking the color barrier by bringing African-American Jackie Robinson into the major leagues. It earned him a spot in the *Baseball Hall of Fame*.

Rickey offers this as his recipe for success, "Success is where preparation meets opportunity." A simple formula that reminds me of the old joke: "How do you get to Carnegie Hall?" The answer: "Practice. Practice. Practice." Obviously, you can't take advantage of an opportunity if you don't have the skills. It's a good recipe for success, but it doesn't reveal the secret main ingredient.

A funny old song from Frank Sinatra gets us little closer to the answer. Do you remember these lyrics from *High Hopes*?

Just what makes that little old ant
Think he'll move that rubber tree plant
Anyone knows an ant, can't
Move a rubber tree plant!

I love that song because a stanza later we learn the ant CAN: "*Oops there goes another rubber tree plant.*" Is having "high hopes" the secret ingredient? No, but it gets us closer to it. You see, the ant succeeds because he doesn't know that he can fail.

Wisdom in the Weirdest Places

Think about some of the people you know who are successful. What is it that makes them big achievers? What traits do you associate with them?

When I ask this question of my audiences I frequently hear the following ingredients: Courage, Perseverance, Enthusiasm, Discipline, Confidence, Decisiveness, Self-reliance, Responsibility, Focus, Ambition, and Optimism.

All of these are certainly traits of successful people, but which one is the overriding characteristic? Which one is the main ingredient?

None of the above!

That's right – none! Yes, they are all important, but there is one ingredient that makes the cake, and that is simply your *belief* that you will succeed. It's called *Self-Efficacy*. Your belief in your ability to achieve what you seek is the biggest part of actually getting there. The best part is that self-efficacy is a trait that can be acquired at any age.

We acquire a sense self-efficacy in four ways. The first way is cumulative. With each success we achieve we add a new layer of confidence in ourselves. The second way is through observation. When we see someone similar to ourselves succeed, we realize that we can too. The third way is controlled by our attitude. A positive attitude enhances our belief in our abilities whereas a negative one destroys it. The fourth way is from the encouragement of others who believe in our ability to succeed. This is where you as an effective manager can help your people succeed. Tell them that you believe they can meet their goals and you will help them believe it too.

Question for discussion or continued thought:

Which of the four ways have you acquired self-efficacy?

Robert Evans Wilson, Jr.

Copy Cats Climb the Ladder of Success Faster

Sometimes observing another doing it is enough

In my last article, *The Main Ingredient*, I wrote about *Self-Efficacy* which is our belief in our ability to achieve what we set out to accomplish. I wrote about how it is the biggest part of achievement, and that we acquire a sense of self-efficacy in four ways: personal experience, observation of others, a positive mental attitude, and from the encouragement of others. This month I'd like to expand on how observing other people achieve motivates us to accomplish more.

Some of our goals require us to reach a mental threshold; some are more physical; while others are a combination of the two. One of my favorite forms of exercise and recreation is mountain biking. I get out once a week and hit the trails. Some of the trails have obstacle course-like obstructions called technical features; they are basically log and rock piles you ride over for an additional skill challenge. One trail has several advanced features including a seesaw. I rode past this particular challenge for weeks; wanting to do it, but frankly too scared to try.

Then one day I encountered another rider who rode across it. He went up to the center; it tipped and he rode down the other side. It looked easy enough, and so I asked him about it. He told me there was one trick to it. You needed to brake slightly when you hit the center, so that your weight would cause the 'up" end to tip down. If you didn't; it would function like a big ramp and you would fly off the end five feet off the ground. Hmm, good advice, because that was definitely what I didn't want to do.

Having seen someone do it; I was ready to tackle it. I rode across perfectly on the very first try. All I needed was to see it done.

We do this all the time -- sometimes consciously and sometimes unconsciously.

A few summers ago I was shopping at Dick's Sporting Goods in Atlanta where they have a three-story in-door climbing wall. My nine year old son was with me and asked to climb it. I bought him a ticket and the rock wall staff strapped him into the safety ropes. He went up about 12 feet and said he couldn't go any further. I was surprised because he is very athletic and picks up most sports immediately and effortlessly. I tried all sorts of encouragement, but he had made up his mind. The staff lowered him to the ground.

Then he asked me to climb it. I looked up and grimaced... it was not what I wanted to do that day, but I had done it once before with my older son, so I paid my way and started to climb. I climbed to the top and rang the bell, then enjoyed the real fun of repelling back down. Once I was down, my son wanted to try it again. I was skeptical and didn't want to waste another two bucks. But, I gave in, and this time he scrambled like a lizard all the way to the top and rang the bell. Just like me and the bicycle seesaw, all he needed was to see that it could be done. Then he was on his way. Of course I'm totally refusing to acknowledge the unstated thought in his mind... "Hey, if my wimpy Daddy can do it – it's gotta be easy!"

Think of the occasions where you found a role model to show you "how it's done."

I remember the night I decided to become a professional speaker. I was serving as a counselor to a group of teenagers attending a *Hugh O'Brian Youth Foundation* leadership seminar. Patty Kitching was the dinner keynote speaker. She was warm and funny and told wonderful stories to illustrate her points. Most of all she looked like she was having the time of her life. I turned to my wife and said, "I could do that. I want to do that!" Three years later, I was.

Go out and find someone who is already doing what you want to do. Watch them, talk to them, and then get started!

Question for discussion or continued thought:

Who can you observe that will help you move your business to the next level?

Robert Evans Wilson, Jr.

Attaboy!

Recognition doesn't have to be tangible to be effective

Seventeen years ago, I became the president of my community association. It was a lively organization with scores of activist members who were busy gentrifying an inner city neighborhood. One of my responsibilities was to deliver a monthly speech and conduct a formal meeting with a loud and raucous crowd.

Over the course of my two year stint, I always spoke from behind the lectern with my hands firmly attached to the sides in a white knuckle grip as I read from my notes. When my term ended, I felt that I might have been a more effective leader if I had some real speaking skills, and if I wasn't so afraid of being in front of an audience.

So, I joined a Toastmasters club and began my training as a public speaker. A year later, I had completed ten speeches and the basic program, but I was still firmly attached to both the lectern and my notes. My mentors encouraged me to work without notes and to move away from the lectern. "At least stand to one side of it!" they cajoled. But I was not about to leave my comfort zone. I was plenty uncomfortable just giving a speech. Besides no one could see my legs shaking behind the lectern.

Then the club held a speech contest. A humorous speaking contest. Now, I can tell jokes, so I was game! Four of us entered the competition, and I managed to win the third place ribbon without venturing an inch beyond the safety of the lectern. I can't recall who placed second, but I'll never forget the winner. Les Satterfield talked about an airplane flight and he soared about the room with his arms spread wide and the audience roared in laughter at his comic yarn. Later on, as I watched him receive his shiny gold statuette for First Place, I knew I had to have one. I was motivated... but not quite enough.

The next contest was for a motivational speech. Once again, I sought refuge behind the lectern. I managed to win the second place ribbon, but the gold went to Doris Posey who moved about the room and interacted with the audience.

I finally took First Place with the Tall Tales contest. I wrote my speech then practiced, practiced, practiced. On the day of the competition -- I did it -- I stepped out from behind the lectern! I told how I would pretend to be Tom Hank's younger brother whenever I flew first class, and how much fun it was to fool my fellow passengers, that was until the time I sat next to his mother.

I loved the recognition that came with that First Place trophy. It motivated me to go further; and forced me to get better. In order to win at higher levels within Toastmasters, I had to develop excellent speaking and speech-writing skills.

I went on to win 13 contests. Years later, when I was hired to give my first professional speech, I wondered whether or not I was truly worthy of getting paid to speak. As I began to have doubts, I looked at those 13 gold trophies in my office bookcase. They represented the acknowledgment that I was indeed worthy.

A few years ago, I visited successful professional speaker, David Greenberg, in his home. I smiled in understanding as I saw, prominently displayed in his living room, several Toastmaster contest trophies.

Recognition doesn't have to be tangible to be effective. A clap on the back, a verbal "Good Job!" in front of peers and co-workers, or a blurb in the company newsletter works too. Even so, nothing works quite as long or as powerfully as something hard and shiny with a name engraved on it. However, you don't want someone resting on their laurels; to keep them motivated, put a date on those plaques and trophies. Then encourage them to renew it every year.

Question for discussion or continued thought:

Who can you give recognition to that will motivate them toward greater achievement?

Criticism Sucks

*Subtle criticism hurts as much as
getting ripped a new one*

"Let me drive the boat."

It was the one statement from the Creative Director that I'd come to dread. It usually came within moments of his reading over my shoulder as I wrote advertising copy on my computer.

It meant, "Get out of your seat; I'm going to start changing your work."

The changes were seldom significant; he never modified the meaning or the motivation of my message. He never altered my concept or idea, but his little edits still sent a powerful message: my work was not good enough to leave alone.

Gradually, over the months I worked for his advertising agency, the constant criticism undercut my confidence. Sometimes it was overt verbal criticism, but most of the time I would simply find that my work had been revised without anyone consulting me. A co-worker suggested that he was simply behaving like a dog, who, had to mark his territory; she said he did the same thing to the graphic designers. I couldn't see it that way - to me - it felt like an attack on my ability.

Before I worked for him full time, I had worked for him freelance. During those days, he praised my work, and constantly asked me to work for him full time. I liked being a freelancer, and was reluctant to take a regular job. Then one day, he made the proverbial offer I couldn't refuse. After that the praise stopped and the criticism began.

Before I took that job, I had won advertising awards, I had been invited by colleges to teach advertising, and I had successfully created ads that significantly increased the revenues of my clients. I was at the top of my game, an authority on advertising, but the almost daily criticism in my new job took its toll.

Sometimes I would write copy that mimicked his style just to see if it would prevent him from changing it. He still changed it. By the time I left that job 18 months later, my confidence was gone. I no longer felt like an authority in advertising. I felt like a failure.

A couple of weeks later, I completed and turned in a new freelance job to a new client. I cringed as he read it - expecting criticism to come at any minute. When he finished, he looked up and said, "This is great! I can't wait to run it."

Relief flooded my body. I hadn't heard those words in so long - they were immediately fortifying - and I felt my confidence returning.

Critics think they are doing us a service; they think they are helping us improve our work, but what they frequently do is destroy our motivation by demoralizing us.

Unbridled criticism given without praise will also destroy relationships. It not only kills self-assurance; it kills love. Whether the recipient is family, friend or lover, the message is clear: "You are not good enough." Some victims of criticism will try to win approbation by changing for the critic, but over time if it is not forthcoming, they will give up.

This funny observation by radio personality Jay Trachman puts relationship criticism in perspective, "Never criticize your spouse's faults; if it weren't for them, your mate might have found someone better than you."

There is a place, of course, for criticism; it is part of teaching. So, if you must criticize, be sure to lace it heavily with praise before and after you give it. In order to motivate someone to become better, remember the *sandwich formula*: Praise - Critique - Praise.

Newspaper editor, Frank Atherton Clark, got it right with this wisdom, "Criticism, like rain, should be gentle enough to nourish a man's growth without destroying his roots."

Question for discussion or continued thought:

How has criticism affected your life?

Robert Evans Wilson, Jr.

More Powerful than You Know

The least bit of praise can be powerfully motivating

"Writing is not a job; it's a hobby!" thundered my father when I told him my plans for college. "You need to get a profession: medicine, law, engineering or accounting."

I cheerlessly acquiesced and enrolled in a Pre-Med program, but at the end of my first year, after struggling through Chemistry, I changed my major to Philosophy. When I told Dad, he grunted, "That and a dime will get you a cup of coffee." He passed away shortly after that but his words echoed in the back of my mind for years.

After graduation I searched for a job in writing. At the same time, I wrote short stories like crazy, and sent them off to dozens of magazines. Years passed and I failed to find a job in writing, so I supported myself by waiting tables and bartending. Meanwhile, rejection letters from the magazines began piling up, and I was beginning to get discouraged.

Then one day, I met a friend for a beer in a bar near the campus of my alma mater. When I visited the restroom, some graffiti written on the wall with an arrow pointing to the toilet paper dispenser caught my eye. It read: *Bachelor of Arts degrees – take only one, please!* Rather than laugh, I grimaced and thought, "Boy, does that sound like my Dad."

Five years had gone by, and other than a few freelance jobs writing advertising copy, I had not made a penny from writing. I was beginning to re-think my life, when I recalled the encouraging words from my ninth grade English teacher.

She had assigned my class with several essays to write. I remembered the glowing paragraphs of praise she wrote in bright red ink at the top of all my papers. There must have been a dozen of those compositions, and just recalling them gave me hope. I thought, "At least one person in the world believes in my writing."

It was just the encouragement I needed, and I doubled my efforts to find work. Soon I was getting a great deal more freelance work. Enough that I was able to quit working in restaurants. Enough to make a down payment on a house. Then whenever I needed a boost in confidence, I would think again of those dozen glowing paragraphs of praise written in bright red ink at the top of my essay papers.

Suddenly everything seemed to gel. I sold my first book; I won several very important advertising awards; and three colleges were asking me to teach a class in copywriting. I was feeling very grateful and once again thought of my ninth grade English teacher and those glowing paragraphs of praise written in bright red ink. I decided to look her up and give her a call.

When I got her on the phone my first shock was that she did not remember me. I was certain I had been one of her favorites. My second was when she told me that she never wrote paragraphs of praise. "There were simply too many papers to grade to write more than a word or two," She said. "I would write 'Nice Work' or 'Good Job,' but never anything more."

Unconvinced, when I got off the phone, I went up to the attic and dug out the box that held my old school work (yes, it's true – I'm a total pack rat – especially when it comes to things I've written!). It took a while, but I finally found those old papers. She was right; there were no paragraphs. And, there was far less than a dozen – only two. About the only thing I remembered correctly was the bright red ink. I did, however, rate more than one or two words. On the first one she wrote, "Nicely written – well thought out." On the other, "Good Sense of Humor!"

Nine words. Nine little words that were so heartening that over the next 15 years they grew into hundreds in my mind. Nine words that motivated me to stick to my dreams. My point? Even the least bit of praise can be powerfully motivating. So, don't keep it in – use your power!

Question for discussion or continued thought:

Where can you use your power of praise?

Robert Evans Wilson, Jr.

Chill Out

The trick is to take your mind off the prize

  The boys slumped against the wall of the dugout; you could read the despair on their faces. "What's the point?" mumbled the right fielder, "We're just going to lose again." The team was on an eight game losing streak, with a record of 3 & 8 and five games left to play.
  As the coach for the nine-year old *Little League* Orioles, I was frustrated. We had some of the finest talent in the league including the best pitcher and the best hitter, but the boys had already given up. I thought, "What can you do when there is no hope of winning?" It was then that I remembered one of the biggest upsets in figure skating history.
  I squatted down in front of them and said, "Lean in, boys, I want to tell you a story about a 16 year old girl who got to go to the 2002 *Winter Olympic Games* as an ice skater."
  "Her name is Sarah Hughes and she barely made the team. She was one of the youngest members, and she would be competing against the biggest names in figure skating - women who had already won world titles. No one expected her to win. No one expected her to even place in the top three. Sarah wasn't expecting to win either."
  "So," I asked the boys, "what is the point of competing when you know you cannot win?"
  "Well, it would be pretty cool just to be in the Olympics," offered the first baseman.
  "And, that's what Sarah thought." I replied. "She was just thrilled to be there; and she made it her goal to simply do her best and have fun. When it was her turn to skate, she chose to do some of the hardest spins, jumps and footwork that an ice skater can do. Why not, she thought, because no one expected her to win. There was no pressure on her to win, and because there was no pressure she did all of those difficult moves perfectly."
  "After Sarah skated, all the big name skaters took their turns. Each one of them tried the difficult moves, but each one was nervous - trying too hard to win - and each one made mistakes. They fell on the ice. And, you can't fall down in the Olympics and win. In the

end, only Sarah skated without falling down, and she won the gold medal."

"Sarah won, because she didn't believe there was a chance for her to win. She went out on the ice to have fun. Boys, that is where you are today. You no longer have to worry about winning. Our record is so bad, that even if we win the next five games, we still won't place first, second or even third. So, what is the point of playing? The point of playing right now is to have fun. There is no pressure on you anymore. I want you to go out on the baseball field today and just have a good time."

They went on to win that day. In fact, they won the last five games. The boys finally started playing at their full potential. At the end of the season, as we entered the playoffs, the top three teams were looking nervously at the Orioles. I'd like to tell you we placed in the playoffs, but once again with the pressure back on, the Orioles choked and got knocked out in the first round.

The trick is to take your mind off the prize, and focus instead on enjoying the project at hand. We've all heard: "It's the journey, not the destination." There is a lot of truth in that cliché. The idea being that we should experience the task as an end in itself. Poet, Crystal Boyd, said it best in her book, *Midnight Muse*: "Work like you don't need money, Love like you've never been hurt, And dance like no one's watching."

Question for discussion or continued thought:

How has the pressure to succeed kept you from achieving your goals?

Robert Evans Wilson, Jr.

Don't Hold Back!

If you believe you can - then STOP over-thinking it

I sat astride my banana seat bike in a parking lot and stared down a thirty foot strip of pavement. It was six inches wide and lined with rubber balls. I was nine years old and participating in a bicycle rodeo. The objective was to ride the entire length without hitting a single ball. The slightest bump would send them rolling.

Nearly a hundred kids had entered, and so far no one had done this event perfectly. Each contestant got three tries. The best hit only five balls, most hit dozens. I didn't see the difficulty. It looked easy, and as it turned out, for me, it was. I did it on my first attempt. No one else was able to do it - even with three tries. I was able to do it for the simple reason that I believed I could.

Decades later, riding my mountain bike, I attempted to ride a 20 foot length of six-inch board that was elevated 12 inches off the ground. I was lucky if I could complete the length one try in twenty. That measly 12 inches of doubt shattered my belief system. As Henry Ford said, "If you think you can or you think you can't, you're right."

We've seen sports stars whose belief system took them to the top of their game: Michael Jordan swooshing the net for a lifetime average of 30 points per game; Tiger Woods routinely sinking impossibly long putts of 50 feet or more; and Babe Ruth pointing to the outfield fence where he would hit a home run. What is their secret? Other than the thousands of hours of practice, which many lesser players also have, each of these men visualized what they wanted to achieve then allowed themselves to do it. Their belief put them "in the zone." When our belief is strong enough, we will succeed. Or as Buddha put it, "We are what we think. All that we are arises with our thoughts. With our thoughts, we make the world."

Is there something you believe you can do, but you've never tried? Many years ago I was president of my neighborhood association. Each month I had to give a brief speech that amounted to little more than giving announcements. Nevertheless, it made me extremely nervous and I clung to the lectern in a white-knuckle grip as I read my notes out loud.

Wisdom in the Weirdest Places

During that time, I participated as a counselor to a group of teenagers attending a *Hugh O'Brian Youth Foundation* leadership seminar. The Saturday night dinner keynote speaker was entertaining and informative; she was also relaxed and clearly having fun. I remember thinking to myself, "I can do that. I want to do that!" In those two succinct sentences I made a belief statement and a desire statement, both of which are necessary for success.

I genuinely believed that I could speak professionally because I had told many a good story across a dinner table, but at the same time I remembered how I felt speaking to the neighborhood association with a stomach full of butterflies. To combat those feelings I joined a Toastmasters club and learned what I didn't know about public speaking.

It took me a year before I could break free of the lectern and my notes. Two years after that I started speaking professionally. I gave presentations on advertising which is the industry I've worked in most of my life, but more than anything I wanted to speak on innovation and creativity.

During my first year or two of speaking, I met a nationally known professional speaker. He asked me what topic I spoke on and I replied, "Creativity." He scoffed at that and said, "There's hundreds of guys speaking on that - you need to find your own niche." On that advice I developed some additional topics, but soon found that the presentation which led to the most recommendations was the one on creativity. What was the difference? It is a subject that I am passionate about. Creative thinking has improved my life time and time again, and it is my belief that it will help others. When I speak on it, I am in the zone.

Is there a business you believe you would be successful in? You would not be dreaming about it - seeing yourself doing it - if you didn't believe you could! Michael Jordan didn't become a basketball star without developing the skills he needed first. He took as many as 2000 practice shots a day to imprint those skills into his mental and physical circuitry. Perhaps all you need is practice.

If there is something you want to do, but haven't tried, then break it down. What parts of the business do you believe you can do? What parts do you believe you can't do? Do the parts you can do outweigh the ones you can't? If yes, then you're off to a good start, and the odds are in your favor. But if the opposite is true, don't let that stop you. Belief must be supported by desire. If your desire is strong enough, you will gain the skills and subsequently the self-belief you need to succeed.

Once you've identified the parts you can't do, ask yourself, "Can I learn to do them?" If not, hire someone else who can. Perhaps you don't even know which parts you don't know. That's OK; hire a consultant, or talk with someone who has already succeeded at this or a similar business. Delegating what you can't do, frees up your belief system and enables you to focus on what you can.

When you believe you can do something - you don't really think about it - you just do it. It's the thinking about it that sometimes holds you back. According to David Eagleman, in his book *Incognito: The Secret Lives of the Brain*, if you're getting trounced in tennis, ask your opponent how they are able to serve so well. He says that will cause them to start thinking about how it is done to the point that they won't be able to do it anymore. Are you over-thinking your desire?

In my research of creative thinkers and innovators, the one trait I found that was nearly universal among them was the belief that they will succeed. They believe they will be able to create whatever it is they have set out to create. They believe they will be able to solve the problem they are facing. Thomas Edison may have expressed it best, "I have not failed 700 times. I have not failed once. I have succeeded in proving that those 700 ways will not work. When I have eliminated the ways that will not work, I will find the way that will work."

What are you waiting for - if you believe you'll succeed - you will. Go for it!

Question for discussion or continued thought:

What abilities do you have where your belief system always allows you to succeed? How can you apply that system to other areas of your life?

CHAPTER NINE - ADVERSITY

In this chapter, I discover the wisdom that is hidden in a run of bad experiences; I get it from a chicken farmer mired in a disgusting task; and from two guys who learn how to turn a crisis into an opportunity.

We will always be faced with adversity whether it is a minor irritation or a major catastrophe. How we perceive it will make the difference in how it affects us. In the following pages, we will observe how some famous people have dealt with misfortune and hard times.

We will also look at how ordinary people have dealt with their troubles and hardships. Problems abound, but when do you seek help? You seek it as soon as you feel yourself falling. I share a heartrending story of a woman who waited until it was almost too late.

Next we'll examine pain. We'll look at both physical and emotional pain and how each can motivate us or shut us down.

Finally we'll look at how to get unstuck. How difficulties can bog us down in depression if we don't perform a vital first step. Alternatively, we will see how problems can stimulate creative thinking. Adversity actually creates opportunities if we're willing to open our minds and seek new possibilities.

Robert Evans Wilson, Jr.

Will You Freak-Out or Hunker Down?

How do you handle a crisis?

Sometimes motivation is forced upon us. We are thrust into the un-comfort zone. And, whether we sink or swim depends on how we respond to the situation. How do you react during a crisis?

Here are the stories of two men who faced a crisis late in life and how they dealt with it. One was a restaurant owner; the other a janitor. The former went into bankruptcy at an age when most people retire, and the latter was fired from a job he'd had for nearly 20 years.

The restaurant owner enjoyed a successful business in a small town at the edge of the Appalachian Mountains. It was a great location along busy U.S. Route 25. And, because he offered the best food and service around, his eatery was jammed from sunup to sundown. But it wasn't to last.

The janitor started his job at St. Peter's Church in London as a teenager. Over the years he married and raised a family and enjoyed a perfectly predictable profession with solid job security. That is until the new vicar came along.

Over the course of 26 years, he was honored by the state governor for his recipes; and was praised by famous restaurant critic, Duncan Hines, in his column *Adventures in Good Eating*. Then things changed. In 1956, the new super highway bypassed the little town. It's amazing the difference just a few miles can make. Two years later the restaurant was closed and the property auctioned off to pay creditors. At 64 years old, the restaurant owner was broke.

It was around the turn of the twentieth century when the new vicar, a stickler for decorum, took over St. Peter's Church. When he learned that the janitor could not read, he gave him three months in which to learn. Quite depressed by the news, the man thought it might make him feel better if he smoked a cigarette.

Unable to afford the cost of opening another restaurant closer to the highway, he reviewed his assets. All he had left was his knowledge and the delicious recipes that made his food so popular. So, he got into his car.

As he walked home, the janitor searched for a tobacco shop. There was usually one on every block, but there were none near the church. He walked block after block without finding one. By the time he reached his house he knew exactly what he was going to do.

Town by town, he drove, stopping at every restaurant along the way. He told the owners they would be more successful if they served his secret recipes under his brand name and paid him a royalty. Two years later, in 1960, he had 400 restaurants serving his food. By 1963 he was making a profit of $300,000 per year. And, in 1964, Colonel Harlan Sanders sold *Kentucky Fried Chicken* to investors for $2 million, plus a lifetime salary of $75,000 per year.

With his meager savings, he opened a tobacco shop near the church. It was an immediate success. His profits went to open a second, then a third and before long he had thriving tobacco shops all over London. Ten years later, he met with his banker about investing his earnings. The banker gave him some papers to sign. The man asked the banker to read the papers to him, explaining that he didn't know how. Shocked, the banker exclaimed, "You are so successful, just think where you'd be today if you could read!" Albert Edward Foreman smiled and sighed, "I'd be the janitor at St. Peter's Church." (Based on a true story by Somerset Maugham)

Did you know that in Chinese, the symbol for the word *crisis* is the same symbol used for the word *opportunity*? Two sides of the same coin. In other words, it's all in our perspective. Will you find the opportunity in your next crisis?

Question for discussion or continued thought:

What crises have you turned into opportunities?

Robert Evans Wilson, Jr.

Thrown into the Driver's Seat

*When leadership is needed,
will you rise to the occasion?*

On June 29, 1863, a 23 year old First Lieutenant received an unexpected promotion. The freckle faced, strawberry blonde, who graduated at the bottom of his class at West Point, was elevated directly to the rank of Brigadier General in the Union Army. He completely skipped over the traditional ranks in between of Captain, Major, and Colonel. As you can imagine such a promotion was met with skepticism, dismay, and envy by his former peers and superiors. Especially at a time when the South was winning against the North during the American Civil War.

Major General Alfred Pleasonton, who promoted the boy, saw his gamble put to the test just four days later in the Battle of Gettysburg. The young general was put in charge of the Michigan Cavalry and tasked with keeping Confederate General Jeb Stuart from attacking the Union Army's rear.

Was he up to the task? Could he keep that dubious star on his shoulder that so many wanted removed? Motivated by the desire to prove himself, George Armstrong Custer, his gleaming saber outstretched in front of him, led the cavalry charge and held the Union line. His successful leadership served as a crucial contribution to the battle that was the turning point in the North winning the war.

When leadership is thrust upon us, many of us are motivated to rise to the occasion. Sometimes, however, leadership must rise in a vacuum. What motivates us to become leaders when there are none?

A few years ago, five friends and I went white water rafting for the very first time. We went on the upper Ocoee River in Tennessee where the rapids are rated Class Four. Not exactly the best choice for beginners, but we had a competent guide, who gave us plenty of instructions on when and how to paddle. He was so good that we were the only rafters in a group of ten rafts that did not capsize and get soaked.

Then halfway through our trip, we went over a small waterfall. When our rubber raft hit the bottom it bent in the middle and folded up like a book. When it sprung back apart our guide was catapulted from the boat and landed several feet behind us. As our leaderless raft sped forward, getting further and further away from our guide, five of us thought, "Uh, oh, what are we going to do!" Before we could panic, my friend Bill started barking commands, "Left side four strokes! Right side two strokes!" With great relief we followed his orders and within minutes he had us safely out of the rushing white water and into the calmer water by the river bank where our guide was able to catch up to us.

A leadership role can jump start motivation. When you have the responsibility of guiding others, it forces you to guide yourself first. I have found that volunteering for leadership roles at work and for non-profit organizations to be self-motivating. Back in the early 1990's, I had a particularly bad year. My mother passed away, a business venture failed, and I had a falling out with my best friend. Needless to say, I was in a funk, and seriously needed something to move me out it. That's when I learned that my community association needed a new President. It was a huge job with a two year commitment that required fund raising, event planning, managing several committees, and supervising dozens of volunteers. It consumed tons of my time, but it also taught me that I could do more in a day than I ever knew. During that same two year period, I launched two new businesses both of which became success stories.

As a manager, you can motivate your employees (or your volunteers) by giving them a mantle of leadership. Suddenly he or she will no longer be just another disaffected cog in the wheel. But with a position of responsibility, those persons will be empowered to do more and be more. Sure, it may require a greater effort on your part, but you will challenge their minds, expand their abilities, and imbue them with a sense of accomplishment.

Question for discussion or continued thought:

Is there someone in your company or family that you can give more responsibility to encourage their leadership abilities?

Robert Evans Wilson, Jr.

Bouncing off the Bottom

*It is human nature to go backwards
before going forward*

"You are going to die," Burt told Valerie after she said she wanted a divorce (I have changed their names to protect the families involved.). The 26 year old policeman lifted a rifle and pointed it at her face.

"No. Please no!" begged Valerie.

Ignoring her pleas and the tears streaming down her cheeks, Burt continued to aim the gun at a point right between her eyes.

After years of abuse; Valerie knew he was serious. She had endured being thrown against walls, choked, slapped, punched, kicked, and spit on. He would pin her against the floor using painful arm twisting techniques he'd learned as a cop for controlling unruly prisoners. On several occasions Burt even dragged her out of bed in the middle of the night, dumped her in the front yard, and then locked her out of the house.

The seconds ticked by like minutes, as she stared into the muzzle of the gun. Completely paralyzed by fear, she was unable to run or even move. Burt pulled the trigger.

Valerie heard the hammer fall, "Click." The chamber was empty.

Burt laughed out loud. He laughed so hard that he fell backwards into the wall.

It was in that moment Valerie felt her love for Burt finally die. Unfortunately, now she was afraid to leave him. It wasn't only fear that kept her married; it was two children; her religious beliefs; and the fact that Burt was so charming she didn't think any of her friends and family would believe her enough to support her decision.

Ten years passed. During that time the abuse continued, but Valerie was afraid to report it. Burt was well liked by his fellow police officers, and he was always careful never to leave marks or bruises. He even warned her, "If you ever try to report me, they will believe me because you don't have any evidence. And, after they leave, you will have to deal with me." She understood that part completely.

The marriage finally ended, but only because Burt decided to leave. Despite being free from abuse, Valerie felt like a complete failure. "If the person who knew me the best was no longer willing to stay married to me, then I must be worthless." It was this feeling of finally hitting bottom that motivated Valerie to make changes in her life.

She began with therapy where she learned that it was Burt who was responsible for his behavior and not her. As her emotional strength grew, she gave back by volunteering at shelters for abused women. In time, her confidence and creativity grew and Valerie became a serial entrepreneur starting several businesses. Today she is the owner of a successful catering business, and married to a kind man who treats her well.

We've often heard the saying, "You've got to hit bottom before you can start to rise again." I have more often than not heard this in reference to alcoholics and drug addicts, but many of us find our lives in a downward spiral, and the problem is that we don't know how to change directions.

As I will mention later in this chapter in the article: *Don't Get Stuck in Reverse*, it is human nature to go backwards before going forward. We revisit wells of happiness that have dried up in the hopes that they might refill.

The downward spiral sucks your energy and ambition, destroys your creativity, and it paralyzes you so that you cannot see new opportunity. It makes you depressed in a way that you don't even know you are depressed. Some people are able to endure an enormous amount of pain before motivation kicks in.

Hitting bottom means that you have gotten so deep in the uncomfort zone that circumstances force you to make changes that you were unable to make for yourself.

The truth is you don't have to wait that long to find the motivation to change. You are already aware that your life is not as good as it used to be. That's all you need to know. The time to ask for help is now.

Question for discussion or continued thought:

Whose counsel would help you turn things around for the better in your business or personal life?

Robert Evans Wilson, Jr.

Is Pain a Motivator?

*I feel your pain; actually, it's mine,
but it helps me understand yours*

The summer of 2013 was the summer that never happened - for me at least. It started out normal enough, maybe a bit too much rain, but I was excited to finally have some warm weather in order to get some work done around the house. I had quite a to-do list... an even longer one for my business.

Then two weeks in, I found myself laid up with both feet injured. It was my own fault, I was invited to play in a Fathers vs. Sons baseball game, and not wanting to embarrass my son, I played hard. Too hard. I woke up the next day with a small pain, which I chose to ignore. I figured I could "tough it out," and I continued on with my daily routines. Instead, I made it worse and the increasing pain motivated me to go see my doctor. I ended up having surgery. For seven weeks I became a prisoner in my home. I was unable to walk or drive, and I became dependent on my sons and fiancée for assistance.

During that time I experienced a lot of pain. I had to keep my feet elevated, braced and iced. Unfortunately, I was unable to fully avail myself of pain medication because I have a low tolerance for it (over-the-counter ones upset my stomach, and the prescription ones put me to sleep). So, for the most part, I had to tough that out too.

Needless to say, all my plans were tabled, and I ended up with a lot of time... time to think. And, perhaps naturally enough, I started to think about whether or not pain is a motivator.

Over the years, as I have written this column, I have often thought that I should address pain as a motivator. However, each time I thought about it, the first image that would pop into my head was *Ben Hurr* chained to an oar in a Roman galley being whipped by the boatswain. Then I thought, "Sure, everybody knows that avoidance of pain is a motivator." And, of course, most of us know that pain is a warning signal to stop doing what you're doing; which, as I mentioned above, I chose to ignore.

Constant pain, however, is not very motivating. In fact, I found it to be quite the opposite. At first I thought, "Good, I can't go anywhere or do anything, I'll be able to catch up on all my writing projects." But, the pain was simply too distracting. I couldn't focus - worse - the pain made me feel so bad that I couldn't muster my usual creative energy. Instead, I found myself doing things that took my mind off the pain like watching television or reading. American humorist, Will Rogers, understood this when he said, "Pain is such an uncomfortable feeling that even a tiny amount of it is enough to ruin every enjoyment."

My pain, or perhaps the weeks of cabin fever, did motivate me toward some long term goals. I decided that once I was better I would take a yoga class to strengthen my joints and tendons, so that this would not happen again. I also researched foods and supplements that would do the same.

The good news is that I didn't suffer from great pain, and I knew all along that it was temporary. But, I started thinking about people who have extreme and chronic pain, and how seriously demotivating it can be. As Samuel Johnson, the 18th century English essayist, once observed, "Those who do not feel pain seldom think that it is felt." Through my own pain, I was beginning to develop some empathy for those who live with it every day.

I recalled my friend Tom, who had his vertebra disks crushed in an auto accident. Several surgeries later, and some serious hardware inserted into his back, his doctor told him he would never be pain free, and would have to take pain medication for the rest of his life.

For seven years he was taking *Oxycontin* for pain, *Klonopin* for sleep, plus muscle relaxers. The drugs took their toll, and six years later he was having extreme mood swings. As an example, he told me how one day while driving he hit a bird and killed it. He started sobbing uncontrollably, then just a few minutes later a driver cut him off in traffic, and he switched to a screaming rage. On top of that his sex drive had completely dried up.

The mood swings and lack of sex drive, drove him to see his doctor. His doctor explained that the pain medication was depleting his testosterone, and jokingly commented, "My nurse probably has a higher testosterone level than you do right now." Tom's wife joined in by adding, "That and you're probably the only man in the world who understands PMS!"

That was it; Tom wanted to get off of the pain medication. His doctor started him on testosterone injections, and switched his pain medication to *Methadone*, which is often prescribed to heroin addicts to help relieve withdrawal symptoms. Tom described to me how he would shave a little bit off of each pill - until over time - he was taking a mere fragment. A year later, he stopped taking it altogether; he was finally pain free, medication free, and sexually active once again.

As I review my summer of pain, in the beginning it took a while, but eventually it motivated me to seek medical attention. The longer term pain I experienced was demotivating and kept me from achieving even my most sedentary goals. On the other hand, it did encourage me to make some lifestyle changes (we'll see how long those last). And, it gave me empathy for people who suffer chronic pain.

I'd like to further explore the motivational factors of pain, so in my next article, I'll write about whether or not psychic pain (emotional pain) drives us to make changes in our lives.

Question for discussion or continued thought:

Do you know someone who suffers chronic pain? How can you help them stay motivated?

Wisdom in the Weirdest Places

The Crash After the Crush

*Intense emotional pain drove me
to discover its true source*

"Look, Daddy, there's a *Taco Bell* at the next exit!"

I grimaced when I saw which exit he was pointing out. My first thought was to say, "No, there are other *Taco Bells* closer to home," but then I thought, "That's ridiculous, I'm not going to let unpleasant memories of my ex prevent me from going into this area of town." I pulled off the interstate.

As I turned onto the familiar road I'd driven hundreds of times during the past two years, an overwhelming sense of gloom descended over my body. Suddenly the joyful afternoon spent with my sons at the movies was gone. The sadness I'd managed to escape for a few short hours was back. The crushing sense of loss settled heavily in my chest; and I was glad I was wearing sunglasses so that my children could not see the tears welling up in my eyes.

I was devastated by the breakup, but I was confused as to why. I was the one who ended the relationship. I had grown tired of the criticism, the manipulation, the lack of respect. I felt like I was doing all the giving, but received little in return. I felt that I could never do enough to please her. More than anything, it was that I still didn't know where I stood with her after two years of dating. One day she'd say she loved me, then the next she would ignore me. It was after a particularly long period of ignoring me that I had enough and ended the relationship.

After I said goodbye, what I never expected - could not anticipate - was the incredible pain that swept over me. I had never felt anything like it before. It was much worse than what I felt after my divorce. And, to top it off, despite all my reasons for leaving her, I still wanted to be with her. That was when I concluded that something was seriously wrong with me. I needed to know why.

I was driven by my severe emotional pain to seek answers, because I never wanted to feel that bad again. I didn't know where to begin, so I set off on what I called a journey of self-discovery. It started with writing in my journal which is how I collect my thoughts and work through problems. As I wrote, exploring my feelings, I noticed that I had a pattern. All of my long term relationships had been with women who had similar personality traits to my ex. How could this be, I wondered. The women I had dated had diverse backgrounds, and vastly different physical appearances.

The next thing I did was read. I searched the self-help section of the book store and bought dozens of books. I was reading some great stuff, but I still wasn't finding what I was looking for. I scoured the web for articles that might give me a clue as to why I was attracted to a specific personality type. I was getting a good picture of the type of person that attracted me, but I still lacked the reason.

After many months, my reading led me to a therapist. My therapist showed me that I was attracted to women who shared my mother's personality traits. I said, "That can't be true, my mother was a wonderful person." What I did not realize was that I was more attracted to my mother's negative traits than her positive ones. My mother passed away 20 years earlier, and I was selectively remembering only good things about her which explained why I had difficulty accepting the bad ones.

In time, I was able to recall physical and verbal abuse I experienced as a child which led to my creating protective behavior patterns that I have followed ever since. My therapist taught me how I acquired, during my childhood years, subconscious beliefs about myself that guided my actions, and had for decades. She also taught me how to change those beliefs.

I was highly motivated by psychic pain to find out why I felt the way I did, so that I could prevent its return. Emotional pain can also cause people to get depressed and shut down. Along my journey, I experienced that too. There were days when my creative energy ebbed, and it was difficult to go to work (see my article: *How to Move Forward* later in this chapter).

Over time, as I studied and came to understand the causes, my pain went away. I learned to recognize women's traits that triggered my old beliefs so that I could avoid them.

Like physical pain, which I explored in my last article, emotional or psychic pain can shut you down or drive you to find a solution. The difference being that the source of psychic pain may be buried in your subconscious and will require a qualified therapist to help you root it out.

Question for discussion or continued thought:

How have you dealt with personal loss, grief, or other emotional pain?

Robert Evans Wilson, Jr.

Don't Get Stuck in Reverse

It's hard to hit a target facing the wrong direction

    I love this quote from Gandalf the Gray, in the book *Lord of the Rings* by J. R. R. Tolkien, "When we despair we cease to choose well. We give in to short cuts." It's so true and we all know that we have been guilty of it at some point in our lives.
    It reminds me of the *Dot Com Bubble* that burst in March of 2000 and caused the stock market to crash, I remember those heady days of "irrational exuberance" as Federal Reserve chairman, Alan Greenspan referred to it. It seemed like everyone was worried they were going to miss out on the digital revolution. They were motivated by the dreams of easy money. It was all about taking a short cut.
    Several start ups approached me to help them promote their new Internet businesses in exchange for stock options. I looked at a couple of cobbled together companies that were little more than a guy with a website and the hopes of mining some venture capital. The idea was to generate web page hits with a clever name or gimmick, sell a ton of stock at the Initial Public Offering, and then retire a millionaire. I decided to stick with those willing to pay in cash.
    After the burst, I read about a repo man in Silicon Valley who repossessed the expensive cars of former Internet millionaires. He reported that he frequently found dozens of losing lottery tickets in the cars -- evidence that the former car owners were acting out of despair and looking for short cuts back to the elusive wealth that had slipped from their grasp.
    Beverly Sills, the famous opera soprano, once said, "There are no shortcuts to any place worth going." But, too often when times are good we pile on the responsibilities. Later on when we encounter adversity, we look backwards instead of forward. We attempt to go back to where we enjoyed success in the past even when it is counter-productive to our current goal.
    In my seminars on innovation I conduct a fun exercise that demonstrates how we frequently feel we must go backwards before we can go forward. A volunteer from the audience is selected and sent out of the room. The audience chooses a simple behavior they

want the volunteer to do (like jumping up and down on their left foot). What makes it fun is that the volunteer must guess the behavior. The audience can only help by saying the word, "yes" when the volunteer does anything that comes close to the desired behavior. They are not allowed to say, "No" or give any other hints.

Once the volunteer performs the desired behavior, the audience rewards it with a round of applause. I ask for a second volunteer, but this time we change the rules after the person leaves the room. When the desired behavior is reached, the audience goes silent, says nothing, and gives no applause. Since the volunteer is no longer getting feedback in the form of "yes" he or she will go back and repeat behaviors that did elicit a "yes." The audience, however, remains silent.

As we watch the volunteer, we can see despair forming on his or her face. The volunteer will then go further backward to find a previous behavior that generated success. Eventually the volunteer quits going backwards and starts initiating brand new behaviors in the hopes of regaining another, "yes." It is after several new behaviors are performed that the audience is signaled to applaud and reward the volunteer for his or her efforts. The purpose of the exercise is to force the volunteer to backtrack to the point that they realize success can only be found by moving forward.

In life, the trick is to stay focused even when our luck seems to be changing. We may have to slow down or make changes in our methods, but the goal must remain the same. Henry David Thoreau observed, "We rarely hit where we do not aim." In other words, if you're moving backward you are moving away from your goal... and it's hard to hit a target when you're facing the wrong direction.

Question for discussion or continued thought:

Do you have a goal that was fallen out of your sites? What can you do today to get back on target?

Robert Evans Wilson, Jr.

STOP Bugging Me!

Things that irritate you are very motivating

    The stench rising off the dead bodies was over-powering. It was so thick you could taste it. Sandy pulled a dust-mask respirator over his face, but the smell still penetrated. To speed up the decomposition process he quickly shoveled manure over the decaying flesh. The manure cut the odor somewhat, that is, if you don't mind the stink of cow dung. Then as he flung each shovelful of waste over the bodies, a black cloud of fat flesh flies would rise into the air. It was a disgusting job that wasted hours of his day, but there weren't many alternatives.

    Sandy is a large scale chicken farmer in the mountains of north Georgia, who prides himself on his clean, well-ventilated chicken houses. He even uses top quality feed, yet despite his best efforts, one to five percent of his chickens die every day. Raising hundreds of thousands of birds at a time presents him with a big pile of dead ones to deal with every day. He tried burying them, but that took up too much land. He tried incinerating them, but that cost as much as $10,000 a month in propane which destroyed his margin of profit. That left composting, but working with rotting carcasses was so gross and annoying that he was determined to find a better way.

    He thought about it for months, but nothing new was coming to mind. Then one afternoon while vacationing in Florida, he took his family to visit an alligator farm. While his kids were squealing in delight at a man wrestling an eight foot long monster, he noticed in another pen that the large reptiles were being fed chickens. Dead chickens. Some of which, in his professional opinion, looked like they had been dead for days. Remarkably these were the ones the beasts ate first. Sandy knew right then how to solve his problem, and he bought a breeding pair of alligators to take home with him.

    Within a few years, Sandy had 400 alligators. He no longer had a dead chicken problem. You might be thinking he had another problem instead: that he was literally up to his elbows in alligators. But when those brutes get to be six feet long, he sells their meat and hides for $200. He now has two businesses that complement each other.

Wisdom in the Weirdest Places

When something bugs you, don't you just want to fix it? We have always heard that *the squeaky wheel gets the oil*. What is annoying you? Things that irritate us are very motivating and also stimulate creative thinking. Is there a task at home or work that you absolutely hate to do? If you can come up with a better way of doing it, you might have a million dollar idea on your hands.

Thomas Stemberg, founder of several successful businesses including *Staples* office supply stores, is a master of million dollar ideas. He once said that he gets his best ideas for starting a new business from being frustrated as a customer. That statement is a roadmap for finding opportunity. Where have you been frustrated as a customer? You can probably think of a dozen places. I'll bet you can fix it. So, don't just sit there - go do it better, and make a million bucks yourself!

Question for discussion or continued thought:

What task irritates you the most? What can you do to fix it?

Robert Evans Wilson, Jr.

How to Move Forward

*You must do this first before
creative thinking will work*

When my wife of 22 years left me I became paralyzed. I was so depressed that I didn't even know I was depressed. I was relieved that the constant fighting was over, but I had no ambition for life. My usual creative energy was gone, and I was just going through the motions. I was no longer looking to the future; I was stuck in the past and barely functioning in the present. The only thing that kept me going was my children.

I found purpose in coaching their sports teams, and becoming the leader of their Cub Scout pack. Those were actions that gave me a sense of accomplishment; and the feeling that I was still important somewhere. Meanwhile my business was at a standstill.

There were innovations I wanted to bring into my business, but I couldn't seem to implement them. In particular, I wanted to give tele-seminars. They would serve two functions: make my services more affordable to a greater number of clients in a tightening economy; and reduce my travel now that I was a single father. But I couldn't seem to wrap my brain around the steps I needed to take.

I read several how-to articles, I talked with people who had produced their own tele-seminars, and I learned about the equipment necessary to put one on. None of this helped. I finally hired an expensive consultant. In retrospect, he really only showed me what I already knew. It seemed that the very act of spending a lot of money spurred me to action where nothing else could. Once again I was productive and moving forward. It wouldn't, however, last.

Three years later, I found myself in the same situation once again. Another relationship had crashed and burned; and in the fallout I found that I was paralyzed and unable to be the driving force my business needed to stay afloat.

It was then, that I realized I had failed to take a critical beginning step. It was something I should have known. It was a vital component of creative thinking that I'd been teaching others for years. I failed to identify the problem. Innovation is all about solving problems or satisfying needs; and before you can be creative, you need to know why you should be.

Wisdom in the Weirdest Places

To move forward, whether it is in business or in a relationship, you have to identify what is holding you back. For me, my blocks were both professional and personal. My business and my relationship were so closely intertwined that I didn't realize I had a problem until I got stuck again.

The innovation technique I share with my clients is to accurately and succinctly state the problem; because the better you do this, the faster you will solve it. Unfortunately, I didn't know what the problem was - just that I had one. Nevertheless I was determined to find out what it was, so that I wouldn't have to repeat the cycle again.

I made inquiries, read self-help books, wrote in my journal, and attended therapy before I could identify it. Once done, however, the process of changing seemed easy by comparison. Even though I had only identified the problem (not solved it), my creative energy and ambition were back - which meant I knew I would.

You can't take the first step until you know where the staircase is. Accurately identifying the problem is like turning on the light at the base of the stairwell on a dark night. Now you can start engaging in some creative thinking.

I know many of you are feeling stuck because of our languid economy. Forget the economy for a moment, and change your perspective by asking yourself how you would tackle your problem if the economy were robust. Sure, the economy is a problem, but it is one that is out of your hands. Identify the problem(s) that you do have control over. Which reminds me of the opening line from the *Serenity Prayer*, by American theologian Reinhold Niebuhr, (and you don't have to believe in God to appreciate the wisdom here):

God grant me the serenity
to accept the things I cannot change;
courage to change the things I can;
and wisdom to know the difference.

If you find that much of your time is wasted by depression or anxiety consider these wise words from Lao Tzu, the founder of Taoism:

If you are depressed you are living in the past.

If you are anxious you are living in the future.
If you are at peace you are living in the present.

Until I came across the above passage I wasted many hours ruminating over what could have been; and worried over what might happen. I have learned to live in peace by focusing on the present - in other words - what I can do today, or if necessary, what I can do in the next hour.

Ask yourself, "What can I do right now - however little it may seem - that will move me toward the completion of my goal?" Then once you have identified that task and started it, your depression and anxiety will melt away. Taking even a small step toward your goal will help stimulate your creative thought process, and that in itself, is a move in the direction of identifying your problem.

Innovation and change - moving forward - involve risk. When you clearly identify the direction you need to go, it makes the risk seem less frightening because you can visualize the rewards.

Slow economies are a great time to initiate change because most everyone else is paralyzed. They are hunkering down and waiting for times to get better. It's a perfect time for you to take the lead. Times will get better for you when you work to change the things within your control.

Question for discussion or continued thought:

Do you have a problem in your business or personal life that you need to identify?

Wisdom in the Weirdest Places

This Story has a Happy Ending... I Promise!

*Adversity motivates you to focus on
what is really important*

I was less than two minutes into my sales presentation when the business owner sitting behind his desk, gruffly said, "Get out of here."

I figured someone must have walked into his office and he didn't want us to be interrupted. I turned around to see who it was; there was no one.

He then said, "I'm talking to you salesman; get your @#%*&, and get out of here!"

I suffered a moment of cognitive dissonance, this wasn't making sense. He had given me the appointment over the phone; I had driven nearly an hour to get there, and even paid for parking. I said, "But, I haven't even shown you the benefits of the program yet."

Then he screamed, "Get out of here now, or I'll throw you out!"

He was a big guy, who looked like a TV mobster; and with his heavy Brooklyn accent, I believed he'd break my legs. I scooped up my presentation notebook, and silently left. Welcome to New York City.

I had accepted that job, selling barter club memberships, before I left Atlanta. It was a cool concept I was sure everyone would love: a member put a set dollar amount of his or her goods and services into the barter club bank, which could then be exchanged for the same dollar amount of any other member's goods and services. Unfortunately, six weeks later, I hadn't sold one. People slammed doors in my face, abruptly hung up on my phone calls, and spoke to me more rudely than ever before. Meanwhile, I received no salary, and was working on commission.

The next week, I finally sold a membership, only to be told by my manager that the company had its quota of that type of business, so they wouldn't be paying my commission. No one told me about the quota. Welcome to New York City.

I quit that job and took one in telephone sales. For three weeks I sold personalized ballpoint pens to small businesses. I was paid an hourly wage, plus a small commission. Payday was every Friday. On the third Friday, I showed up for work to an empty office. The company had moved in the middle of the night. I learned from the police that it was a Boiler Room, and they were conducting some sort of phone scam. I had naively worked in one of the straight jobs that made the company look legitimate. I would get no paycheck for that week's work. Welcome to New York City.

Before moving to New York, I made a down payment to purchase a co-op apartment that was under construction. It was supposed to be ready the day I arrived from Atlanta. When the moving truck pulled up, my unit was not finished. The builder assured me it would be ready in one week. I put my belongings into storage, moved in with a buddy and slept on his sofa. One week quickly became eight weeks, so I demanded an inspection of the building. Nothing had been done since the first time I saw it. I had to threaten a law suit to get my money back. Welcome to New York City.

I then rented an apartment for four times what I had been paying in Atlanta. Plus, I had to pay the equivalent of three months' rent to move in: the first month's rent, a security deposit, and a real estate commission. Welcome to New York City.

One night a hit-and-run driver wrecked my parked car. A neighbor got the license plate number when he heard the crash. I called the police. They asked if the neighbor could identify the driver. He could not; he only saw the car driving away. The police then said the car was reported stolen one hour after my car was hit, and unless we could identify the driver they could do nothing. Welcome to New York City.

My girlfriend thought that my becoming a stockbroker would be glamorous, and I wanted to please her. I sent resumes to dozens of firms; I interviewed with several; but I couldn't land a position. I looked for other high-end sales jobs, but couldn't find one. I got depressed, which made things even harder. Then I ran out of money. That had never happened to me before. I was too embarrassed to tell my girlfriend, so I borrowed money from my mother. And, I started looking for the type of job I knew I could get: waiting tables. My girlfriend urged me not to do that, but I was in a panic.

Two weeks later, I had a job in a restaurant, money in my pocket, and for the first time in four months New York City didn't seem evil. I can't help but think of these words from the song *New York, New York*: "If I can make it there, I'll make it anywhere." I wasn't making it; New York chewed me up and spit me out. And, while I'll always love visiting the Big Apple, I was clearly not meant to live there.

I'm sharing this story because the adversity I experienced motivated me to focus on my most important goal. It made me realize I had been wasting my life. I wanted to be a writer, but I wasn't pursuing it seriously. I did not write every day, and I was not trying to get my work published. When I got back to Atlanta, I cashed in a life insurance policy to buy a personal computer. I used it to write eight hours a day; and each week I mailed several query letters to book publishers, or at least one short story to a magazine. I was finally working in the career I had always dreamed of.

If you are experiencing tough times... let them remind you of what is most important in your life. Then let them motivate you to get back to your primary goals.

Question for discussion or continued thought:

How has adversity motivated you to make changes in your life?

CHAPTER TEN – GAINING MOMENTUM

In this chapter, I find wisdom while fishing; from a moment of overconfidence when I thought I could speak a foreign language better than I actually could; and from a guy who would lie to his family in order to spend more time working.

Knowledge is power; we'll look at how it is also motivating. We'll look at how acquiring comprehension and understanding opens new worlds of opportunity.

First we'll examine how it builds confidence, and how it makes taking risks much easier. Then we'll see how it leads to success. Achieving success creates its own motivation and makes us hungry for more.

Finally, we'll see how success builds upon itself, and how it builds momentum that continues to motivate you long after the initial work is done.

Robert Evans Wilson, Jr.

The Examined Life

Knowledge gives you the confidence to take a risk

"Hola!"
"Hola. ¿Qué tal?"
"Bien. ¿ y tu?"
"Bien."

Paul and I were sixteen years old and had taken high school Spanish for a year. We called each other every night on the phone and spoke to each other in our new language. More than anything we wanted to test our skill with a real Spanish speaking person, but we did not know any. Then we got the idea to have dinner at a Mexican restaurant. For two boys who had never dined out without their parents, this was a big adventure. We were so motivated that when we made reservations, we asked to be seated with a waiter who could not speak English.

What motivated us? Knowledge. We made the same discovery that led Sir Francis Bacon to make his famous quote in 1597, "Knowledge is power." We were empowered by what we had learned, and it gave us the confidence to take a risk we would never have taken before.

By the end of dinner we found out we didn't know nearly as much as we thought we did, but the important thing was that our knowledge, albeit meager, moved us to action.

It is the same reason that we find seminars and lectures so motivating -- because we acquire new insights in a relatively brief period of time that we can act on right away. If the information is good, we can't wait to put it to work making our lives better and our jobs easier.

Knowledge also motivates us because it enables us to be more inventive. Many new innovations are the result of two or more existing ideas synthesized into a new one. Creative thinkers regularly expose themselves to new learning experiences, and to different viewpoints. With each new experience, they create new synapses – electrical connections between the nerve cells – in their brains. This gives them more data to draw from when they are looking for solutions.

Wisdom in the Weirdest Places

My son recently asked me why his school required him to learn to play a musical instrument. I explained to him that it was stimulating parts of his brain he would not have used otherwise. I told him that even if he chose not to continue playing the instrument as an adult, that the knowledge he acquired today may serve him in the future in some way that is presently unknown to him.

Innovators are known for their ability to think outside of the box, but more than anything it is their broad-based knowledge that gives them the courage to challenge accepted beliefs. The most successful innovators are those who make the acquisition of knowledge part of their lifestyle.

Greek philosopher Socrates fully understood that learning is a lifelong process. When he was found guilty of teaching his students to question authority, he was given a choice of punishment: death or exile. He chose death, stating, "The unexamined life is not worth living,"

Knowledge, however, is more than just the accumulation of information. It has to be used, applied, and manipulated in some fashion. Automobile manufacturing innovator, Henry Ford, illustrated this point during a civil trial in which he sued a Chicago newspaper for libel. The paper had referred to him as an "ignorant pacifist." At the trial, the defendant's lawyer asked Ford a series of questions designed to prove that he was indeed ignorant. Questions such as "When was the American Revolutionary War?" and "How many soldiers did the British employ?"

Eventually Ford became irritated by the questions and remarked, "I can summon to my aid men who can answer any question I desire to ask concerning the business to which I am devoting most of my efforts. Why should I clutter up my mind with general knowledge?"

Seek out knowledge that empowers you, and let it give you the confidence and courage to be more and do more.

Question for discussion or continued thought:

What special knowledge have you acquired that gives you confidence in your work or hobbies? What additional knowledge would you like to have?

Robert Evans Wilson, Jr.

The First Million

*Seductive and intoxicating,
success breeds more success*

    Until I was thirty years old, I wasn't much of a fisherman. I'd take a rod and reel along on a camping trip, but I never expected to catch much of anything. In my mind, fishing was a relaxing past time you enjoyed with friends and beer. Then my buddy Brian asked me to go fishing. I took him to a lake I knew that was hidden in the woods; and he taught me how to fish for bass. He showed me how to cast my lure along the edge of the lake; how to give the line a couple of tugs to "jig" the lure and attract the fish; then to reel it back in quickly.

    I accepted his instructions affably, but with little faith, then popped open a bottle of beer and started to get into the rhythm of relaxation. Cast, tug, reel. Swig. Cast, tug, reel. Swig. Cast, tug, reel... Whoa! Something hit my line. Hard. Really hard! I'd never felt anything like that before. My line started spinning out of the reel with a high-pitched whining sound. I cranked it back in as fast I as could, but the drag was set too low and the fish was pulling it back out faster than I could turn the handle.

    Suddenly, a hundred feet in front on me, a bright green monster burst out of the lake. It was a large-mouth bass that leaped, full length, out of the water. Shimmering in the sunlight, he shook his head back and forth in an attempt to break free from my hook; then splashed back beneath the surface. I couldn't believe it - it was just like I'd seen on television - and it was happening to me.

    Afraid that I'd lose the fish, I yelled at the top of my lungs, "Brian, Help!" He was nearly halfway around the lake, but he dropped his own rod and charged toward me; yelling instructions all the way. I tightened the drag and reeled the fish in a little, then let him pull the line back out to tire him. It felt like an hour, but was probably less than ten minutes, before I finally got him in. He was 18 inches long and weighed eight pounds. The bass wasn't the only one to get hooked that day; I was too - I couldn't wait to go fishing again!

For the first time in my life, I had experienced fishing success. Success in anything is very motivating. It builds confidence and encourages you to keep pursuing that particular endeavor.

In sales, getting to that first closed deal is critical for getting people to stay in that profession. When I started out in my first sales job, I recall becoming deeply discouraged by hearing "No," over and over again. I mistakenly took the rejection personally, and wanted to give up too soon. I recall the old timers advising me, "It's just a numbers game - you have to get a certain number of rejections before you'll get a sale."

Over time, I realized that was not really accurate. It is only a numbers game in that every single sales attempt is a baby step up the learning curve. You learn how to read body language; and how to listen carefully to what your prospect is telling you about his or her needs. Then from these things you gain clues in how to share your expertise so that your customer has enough confidence to buy from you. Eventually, you go from baby steps to giant steps. Wealthy, successful people have always said, "The first million is the hardest to make."

Question for discussion or continued thought:

When have you experienced success which motivated you to achieve even more?

Robert Evans Wilson, Jr.

Keeping the Ball Rolling

Momentum is the point when success comes easily

    I know an advertising agency owner who never fully takes a vacation. He takes his family to fairly exotic locations, but never so alien that they are outside the reach of modern communication. In other words, he is never further than a cell phone call or email away. He checks in with the office several times a day – much to the chagrin of his family who want him to be fully engaged in the holiday at hand. So, he ends up sneaking off under the guise of visiting the restroom, or going to the bar for a cocktail, in order to connect with his staff, a client or a prospect. His wife and kids aren't fooled; they just sigh and accept the inevitable. I used to think he was a control freak – someone who couldn't let go and let someone else take over – until I came to understand the concept of *Momentum*.

    In science, *Momentum* is equal to *Mass* times *Velocity*. Or just think of Indiana Jones, in *Raiders of the Lost Ark*, running as fast as he can out of the tunnel while that huge stone ball rolls faster and faster after him. In business, *Momentum* is the point at which success begins to come easily. Business veterans jokingly refer to it as having, "paid my dues." In short, momentum is an accumulation of acquired knowledge, skill, experience and connections. And, those who understand it... also know it can be fragile and easily lost.

    Sales professionals who have achieved momentum will tell you that you must pursue a number of activities to generate sales leads: phone calls, emails, sales letters, networking events, etc. You keep it up building dozens, then hundreds of leads at a time. Then to convert those leads to sales you keep following up on each of them in a timely fashion. Meanwhile, you are still maintaining all the activities that continue to generate leads. So between generating leads, following up on leads, then turning leads into sales, you begin to feel like the guy in the circus who spins plates on top of poles – rushing from one plate to the next to keep them spinning.

    No wonder these folks hate to take vacations – it breaks the momentum they've spent months or years creating and they know it takes time to get it going again.

Years ago when I first started giving speeches, a seasoned professional speaker advised me, "It took me ten years to quit sweating cash flow, but even so, it is still all about non-stop marketing." In other words: maintaining momentum.

For a growing company, momentum is the point where you have done enough advertising, marketing, public relations, networking, customer service, and so forth that business begins to flow. It is the point where you are garnering the precious and often elusive *word-of-mouth* referrals. Momentum is about building a reputation. Acquiring it, however, doesn't mean you can taper off on your efforts... but it does mean that your efforts will become easier.

The best thing about momentum is that once you get it, motivation becomes self-perpetuating. Momentum is energizing. It keeps you on your toes. And, the rewards come quickly and regularly.

I have found this to be true in all pursuits. Even when I am writing fiction there is always a certain point in a novel that it takes on a life of its own and demands my daily attention, energy and focus until it is complete. Unfortunately, nothing quite puts the brakes on momentum like finishing a book, or completing any other major task. The trick to avoid losing that momentum is to begin another book or another task before you complete the first one. Then you just shift your energy over to the next project that is already under way.

Question for discussion or continued thought:

What steps are you taking to build momentum in your business?

CHAPTER ELEVEN - EMPATHY

In this chapter, I collect wisdom from a clever client, a gas-can con artist, and a lying advertising agency owner.

We'll look at how relating to people is a powerful way to get them to do what you want; and become converts to your cause.

When you can feel someone's pain, or even their joy, you can connect with them in more meaningful ways. It enables you to communicate more effectively, which in turn will help you motivate them.

Do you want more customers? More friends? Better relationships? Open yourself up to people's feelings, interests, fears and desires.

When you understand another's motivation, you can speak to them from a place that they recognize. When you are aware of what's important to another person, you will comprehend the issues they are dealing with. And, this will enable you to help them solve the problems they are facing.

Robert Evans Wilson, Jr.

Empathy on Empty

Fill up your tank with this business boosting tool

I saw six people huddled on the sidewalk in front of me; through their legs I saw what looked like a body on the ground. I rushed over to see what was going on. I saw a man with a bloody gash on his head; he appeared to be unconscious. I pushed through and started checking him out using my Boy Scout First-Aid training. His clothes were filthy and tattered, and he smelled bad, but a quick examination showed that his wound was not very deep.

I was a nineteen year old college kid, and had just moved into my first apartment. I was walking to get acquainted with the neighborhood, when I found the injured man. "What happened?" I asked the crowd.

"He's a drunk; I'm calling the police!" responded one man.

I couldn't believe the callous response. "This man is hurt," I cried. He doesn't need the police - he needs help!"

I roused the man and got him to his feet. "Come on Mister, let me take you home."

I asked him where he lived. He grunted and pointed down the block, so I took his arm and we started walking. I gave a dirty look to the guy who wanted to call the police. I was clueless that my ward might be homeless.

At each intersection, I asked him which way to go, but he always pointed straight ahead. In the middle of the third block he veered off the sidewalk and into the street where he stopped. Then to my shock, while I was holding him up, he unzipped his fly and began urinating in the middle of the road. I was mortified. I looked around; hoping the guy up the street had not called the police. At that moment, I was glad that none of my neighbors knew me yet.

When he finished, we walked another block. The street ended at a park. I asked the man which way to turn. Suddenly, he developed a burst of energy, broke free from my grasp, ran deep into the park, and disappeared into the trees. I stood there staring after him feeling stupid.

A few years later, I moved to New York City. It was my second week in the Big Apple when I stopped my car at a red light. A man holding a gas can walked up to my window and said, "I live out on

Long Island and ran out of gas, but I left my wallet at the house." He held the can up expectantly and said, "A gallon will get me home."

I was very intimidated by the size and congestion of New York; I knew I would hate to be stuck there without my wallet. I handed him two dollars. Two days later, I pulled up to a red light at a different intersection when the same man came up to me with the same story. I was furious.

After experiencing a few more incidences like these, my empathy was running on empty. Whatever natural compassion I carried from my youth was being ground out daily by the harsh realities of life. As I became more successful professionally, I paid it forward with generous donations and volunteer work. But empathy? Understanding people's feelings? There just didn't seem to be a role for it in my life.

Then one day, I needed a little myself. My love relationship was falling apart. I explained my concerns to my girlfriend in the hope for some understanding, but none was forthcoming. On the other hand, I was too caught up in my own issues to have any feelings for hers. The relationship ended. I was distraught, but it made me determined to learn how to be more empathetic in the future.

As I explore empathy, I have observed that I'm not the only one suffering from a lack of it. It seems to be a worldwide phenomenon. Just like me, people are demanding that they are offered compassion, but take no time to understand the viewpoint of others.

The more I learn about it however, it seems that the opposite would be true, because the benefits of empathy are enormous. For one, it is a great way to motivate people - not just in our personal lives - but in business as well.

California-based graphic designer, Moira Hill, says, "Being empathetic absolutely helps in business - because it allows you to see things from your customer's perspective and adjust your service and how you provide them accordingly." She adds, "Empathy increases kindness in the world. It takes little time, and a small action can have ripple effects."

Hillary Nash is a top seller of cancer insurance policies for AFLAC. She attributes her success to sharing her own story of how her family was devastated by her father's cancer. "I hear from clients often about how they were touched that I would share something so personal."

Psychotherapist and author of *The Self-Aware Parent*, Dr. Fran Walfish, enjoys repeat business and referrals because she tells patients some of her own personal struggles. "I share a flaw of my own to help the patient put into perspective their own challenges and to realize that even the doctor whom they idealize and hold in high regard has problems, too."

Dr. Joseph Shrand, an instructor of Psychiatry at Harvard Medical School, says that good business is based on relationships, and that respect is the first step you take in having empathy for someone. He makes this observation, "When is the last time you got angry at a person who was treating you with respect? You don't!"

Executive coach, Dr. Karissa Thacker, sees it as a business tool. "Nice guys can finish first, if they have an enlightened, practical understanding of empathy."

Does your empathy need a fill up?

Question for discussion or continued thought:

Describe how you can implement empathy into your business or work?

Wisdom in the Weirdest Places

Bleed It Out

*Some advertising is designed to
speak to your subconscious mind*

Half a century ago marketing consultant, James Vicary, pulled a hoax on the American people as a way to promote his advertising agency. He reported that he flashed the words "Drink Coca-Cola" and "Eat popcorn" on the screen for a millisecond during a movie in a theater, and caused large numbers of people to visit the concession stand. He called the effect *Subliminal Advertising*. Subliminal means that the effect functions below the threshold of consciousness. Years later, when others failed to duplicate his results, he admitted that he made the whole thing up. Never-the-less, the myth continues.

So, is there any advertising that does work below the threshold of consciousness? Yes. Much of advertising is clearly designed to speak to you on a subconscious level. Ads are created to get you to relate to the setting; the background music; the age, race and gender of the actors; their clothing; and the activities in which they are involved. The idea is that you will recognize yourself in these people and, in turn, make the connection, "Ah, this is my kind of product." You don't think it... you feel it. And, feelings move us to act.

A few years ago I was involved in non-profit fund-raising for a Christian Mission in Africa. In order to learn what type of appeal would bring in the most money, we conducted a series of focus groups. We asked, "Which would you be more likely to do: A. Give money to feed starving babies; or B. Give money to teach people how to grow drought resistant crops that would end starvation in their community." The answer they gave was almost universally: B. The comments we heard frequently included the proverb: "Give a man a fish and you feed him for a day; teach a man to fish and you feed him for life."

We then tested both appeals. Oops, the focus groups were wrong. The appeal for feeding starving babies won by a landslide. The lesson we learned was that the emotional appeal to save the life of a child is much more powerful than a logical appeal for teaching a village survival skills that would eliminate starvation. From that point forward, the heart-tugging stories of babies dying headlined every ad we ran.

Emotion trumps logic every time. Take for example, Nick Ut's 1972 photograph of a 9-year-old Vietnamese girl who was naked, shrieking and running away from her village that had just been bombed with napalm. Fear, despair and suffering were written all over her face. More than anything it was her complete vulnerability that captured our attention. One snapshot revealed the gut-wrenching horror of war, and millions of people, whose hearts were touched, turned their attention toward ending the Vietnam War.

Perhaps you recall hearing these potent words in a speech by Jesse Jackson back in 1984: "These hands... these black hands... these hands that once picked cotton will now pick presidents." Thrilling words. Exciting words. I remember them well. And, even though I wasn't his target audience, they created a powerful image in my mind, and when he finished, all I could say was, "Wow!" Meanwhile, for millions of African Americans, it was the motivation needed to put apathy aside and go to the ballot box.

We are charged and moved by many emotions. Here are just a few: acceptance, amusement, anger, angst, annoyance, anticipation, arrogance, awe, anxiety, bitterness, calmness, caution, confidence, courage, determination, disappointment, discontent, disgust, desire, delight, elation, embarrassment, envy, excitement, fear, friendship, frustration, gratitude, grief, guilt, hate, happiness, impatience, inadequacy, irritability, inspiration, joy, jealousy, kindness, loneliness, love, lust, modesty, negativity, nostalgia, paranoia, patience, pity, pride, regret, resentment, sadness, self-pity, serenity, shame, surprise, timidity, torment, worry, yearning, and zeal.

Question for discussion or continued thought:

Which emotions from the above list are currently moving you?

Wisdom in the Weirdest Places

Forget the Facts - Tell a Story

*Using narrative to translate
your mission into human terms*

Recently I was asked by the sales manager of a company if I could reach his staff with a message he had been trying to "beat into their heads for months." Uh, his words not mine.

He wanted me to accomplish what he failed to do: inspire his sales people to spend more time pursuing smaller accounts. He said they were all good producers so he couldn't threaten them with job loss, but the company depended on those smaller accounts because they made up the bulk of their business.

His sales staff only wanted to work with the larger accounts because they generated higher commissions. He said, they complained that the small accounts took up too much time, and were not worth it.

They were cold to his logic. In order to convince them, I knew I needed to translate the company's mission into human terms. In short, I needed to come up with a story they could personally relate to.

I did some research to find some good ones. Then I recalled a story of my own, one I had not thought of since the 1980s when I worked as a wholesale apparel salesman. Yes, I was a rag rep. One day at the Miami Apparel Mart, a clothing store owner stopped by my showroom to say she did not have time to shop with me, but asked if I would visit her store on my way back to Atlanta. I agreed.

Having never worked with her before, I did not know what to expect. When I arrived at her shop, I groaned. It was the smallest store I had ever seen. It was maybe 300 square feet. There was barely room to show her my samples. As I looked around the tiny space, I imagined the tiny order I might get. Nevertheless, I patiently worked with her. It took over two hours. When it was over - my prediction came true - I received a mediocre order.

As I drove away, I grumbled to myself about the time I had wasted. But it got worse. The client called me multiple times with changes to her order. She was very demanding and had several special needs. I complied cordially. I was never brusque, but wondered how much more hand-holding this woman was going to need. Even my partner got annoyed seeing me on the phone so often with her; and said, "You need to cut your losses on that account!"

A few weeks later, the store owner visited my showroom at the Atlanta Apparel Mart. This time I ended up working with her for several hours. She wanted to see everything we had. I was patient and polite, and did not rush her, but I grew more irritable by the minute. She took copious notes, thanked me and left. I was furious - all that work and no order to show for it!

A couple of days later, she dropped off the largest order I had ever received. I was dumbfounded. My first thought was that such a small store would not have the necessary credit, and the manufacturers would never ship this amount of merchandise to her. But that was not my decision to make. I placed the order and waited to see what the factors would say. To my surprise the order went through without a hitch.

The clothing was shipped and a week later she re-ordered. Again, I was shocked. Completely baffled, I started asking some of the reps I knew from other manufacturers what they knew about her. I soon learned that she was a maven. She had hundreds of loyal customers who would not get dressed without her fashion advice. The merchandise in her store turned over every week. She had a multi-million dollar business that she started out of her home before she ever rented space in a commercial building.

Later on, she confessed that her first order with me was a test. She wanted to see how I would work with her. I passed. I was so happy that I had been patient with her because she became one of my top customers for a long time.

It worked! I could tell that my client's sales people connected with the story because it generated a lively discussion where several offered similar stories of their own. I then reinforced my message of "hidden gold mines" by sharing another story with them about a colleague who nurtured his fledgling customers to success by sharing his expertise in how to build a business. Because he took the time to help them grow, they became loyal customers.

As I told each story, the sales people imagined similar scenarios where they might benefit from working with their own smaller customers. Annette Simmons, author of *The Story Factor: Inspiration, Influence, and Persuasion through the Art of*

Storytelling, said, "Story is your opportunity to create in your listeners' imagination an experience that feels real."

When you need to persuade, forget the hard facts; instead share a relevant story that touches the heart.

Question for discussion or continued thought:

What value(s) would you like to impart to your staff? What story can you tell them that will illustrate it?

CHAPTER TWELVE - PASSION

In this chapter, I gather wisdom from a tobacco-chewing redneck; from a whirlwind weekend producing a ketchup commercial; and from an idea that I couldn't forget - even after 15 years.

Here I explore passion, and like desire, passion is one of those motivators that move us forward. Passion is an intense emotion that we cannot ignore. It is a very strong feeling about something, whether it is a person, an idea, an activity, a place or an object. And, usually it brings us great joy or satisfaction.

If we are passionate about something, then we have an extreme interest it. We have lots of enthusiasm for it, and we are eager to spend time on it. When we are passionate about something, we are energized by it.

There so many things we might be passionate about: political causes, a sport, art, music, and most likely a lover. I share with you some ideas that I couldn't leave alone. I had to see them to completion.

I also look at the passions of other people. How they offer us a key to what makes them tick, and how they are motivated or often ruled by the things they are passionate about.

I close with a fun look at the motivational value of music.

Robert Evans Wilson, Jr.

Good Stuff also Comes in Threes

*Love is a foundation for confidence,
creativity and growth*

A few years ago I was surfing the internet on a Friday afternoon when I discovered a contest asking amateurs to make TV commercials for a famous ketchup brand. The prize was several thousand dollars and your commercial would actually run on television. Instantly I had an idea for a romantic comedy in which ketchup brought two young lovers together. Romance was on my mind; I had recently started dating someone with whom I was very interested.

Then I read the rules, and swore, "Darn it; the deadline is three days from now!"

In order to make a commercial and enter the contest, I had to get a videographer, a video editor, an actor, an actress, and a place to shoot the video. Plus, I had to write a script that would squeeze into 30 seconds. Then we had to rehearse, shoot, edit, and then upload it to a website on the internet.

The idea was too fun to waste. I could see it perfectly in my head. In a diner, a woman walks over to a table where a single guy is having his lunch. She asks to borrow his mustard and as she reaches for it, he grabs her hand and says in flirtatious way, "You didn't come here for mustard; you came for something else."

Responding in kind, the woman says, "And, what would that be?"

"The ketchup," he says impishly, then squirts some into the palm of her hand and starts dipping French Fries into it.

The woman is shocked and exclaims, "When you let go, you're going to get a face full of ketchup!"

The man smiles and offers her a fry. She then picks up the bottle and squeezes her phone number in ketchup across his arm. She then walking away she says, "Better not let that run!"

An announcer then assures the viewer that this ketchup never runs.

I could feel the creative juices flowing in me, and I was determined to make this commercial. I got on the phone, and was immediately able to kill two birds with one stone by calling my cousin Caroline. She used to be a wedding videographer and now owns a restaurant. She loved the idea and was in. She then recommended a video editor. I called Ivan, and he was in. It took the rest of that day and all of the next to find an actor and actress. In the end, Ivan knew an attractive couple that acted. I called Ed and Shana and they jumped on board. In between phone calls I wrote the script.

    We all got together the next morning. We spent the first half of the day shooting, and the second half editing from all the takes. We were finished by dinner time with hours to spare before the midnight deadline.

    I've encapsulated the events, but for three days I was bursting with creative energy and it felt fabulous. I recall that weekend as the beginning of a long run of creativity, success and joy. I was in thrall to romantic love, and the overflowing energy from it was driving me to create some exciting new speeches and seminars for my business, which in turn was bringing me increased prosperity.

    "Love me and the world is mine," wrote lyricist David Reed in 1906. He is right because when we are in love and that love is returned, we have a foundation of comfort and confidence from which we can innovate and build. When Abraham Maslow developed his *Hierarchy of Human Motivation*, he placed love on the third tier or right in the middle. I know it would be hard to think about love when you're cold and hungry, nevertheless, I'm thinking maybe it should be first - right there on the bottom supporting everything else.

    Psychologist and author Gay Hendricks says that when we expand in love we also expand in creativity and success - the three rise together. I've certainly experienced that, and for me, romantic love might just be the most important motivator of all. Bring it on!

NOTE: The *YouTube* link for the above mentioned TV commercial, *Heinz Gettin Lucky*, can be found here:
http://www.youtube.com/watch?v=BDWeW0RZD3E

Question for discussion or continued thought:

What has romantic love motivated you to do?

Robert Evans Wilson, Jr.

Compelled by an Idea

*Sometimes an idea is so exciting
you can't leave it alone*

    I was leaving my last class for the day when I saw my friend, Ken Frankel, working out in the hallway with one of those pistol-grip label makers. I stopped and asked what he was doing.
    "The Dean asked me to put the room numbers up in Braille so the blind students can find their classrooms."
    As I watched Ken work, I thought of some of the blind students I knew there at Georgia State University. Suddenly the devil got into me and I asked, "Does that thing do the alphabet as well?"
    "Yes." Ken replied.
    "Excellent! Let's take it over to the men's restroom in the Student Center and put up some graffiti in Braille!"
    So we did. The next day we made a point of running into our blind friends, and asking them if they had been keeping up with the graffiti that people were putting up in the stalls.
    The typical answer was, "Come on man, why are you asking me that when you know I can't see it?"
    So we replied, "Next time you're in there, feel above the toilet paper dispenser."
    They did, and within 48 hours every blind student on campus had heard about it. Then they were after us to put up some more! They told us, "This stuff is great!"
    Feeling obligated to get some new material; we hit the bars for inspiration. One night we found the mother lode: the men's room at *Moe's & Joe's*, a 50 year old pub where they never painted over the witticisms scrawled on the walls.
    Several mugs of beer and several trips to the restroom later, we filled several sheets of paper with funny bathroom graffiti to take back with us. As we looked at our collection, we came to two conclusions: first that we'd had way too much beer, and second that we should keep collecting graffiti until we had enough for a book.
    Little did we know how long that would take! After a few days of active searching we had little to show for our efforts. Somewhat frustrated, we made a decision to just collect new material whenever we happened upon it.

Wisdom in the Weirdest Places

A decade passed, but it was an idea I couldn't forget. It still made me laugh every time I thought of it. I kept the idea alive, and we kept collecting. Finally, 15 years later, our collection was big enough and we found a publisher who agreed with us that it was a very funny idea. In the fall of 1996 our book, *OFF THE WALL! The Best Graffiti Off the Walls of America*, hit the bookstores.

Sometimes an idea is so exciting that we can't leave it alone. We have to see it to fruition. I've been compelled by ideas to start new businesses, erect buildings, write novels, and even create new recipes.

My friend Jordan Graye, a radio personality in Atlanta, became energized by an idea when she learned that the actual inventor of radio, Nikola Tesla, never got credit for it in his lifetime. Like many people in radio, she believed that Gugliomo Marconi was the man who discovered it.

As she read more about Tesla, she learned that he was also the inventor of alternating current electricity - the type of electricity that powers our homes and offices. She became incensed that history had forgotten this real-life Prometheus; and made it her mission to remind the world of his gifts.

She thought the best way to restore Tesla's fame would be in a film. That she had never made a movie before (and knew next to nothing about making one), did not deter her one bit.

Jordan did her research and composed a story. She then hired writers, actors, camera operators, and lighting people. She committed her time, energy and a sizable portion of her life savings to realizing her dream. Three years later, *MegaHertz* was complete and Nikola Tesla's life story revived.

What idea is motivating you? Are you working on it?

Question for discussion or continued thought:

What are you passionate about? Is there an idea lurking within you that needs to come out?

Robert Evans Wilson, Jr.

Sometimes You Have to Rip the Cover Off

Discover someone's passion and you'll know what motivates them

On a summer weekend in 1977, my friend Tony and I made plans to go waterskiing. When he picked me up there were two people in the car that I did not know. He introduced his new girlfriend Sue, and her brother Bubba.

Bubba was the quintessential redneck. Within minutes of getting on the boat, he stuffed a wad of chewing tobacco the size of a baseball in his cheek, then chugged several beers. In less than an hour we were dealing with an irritable drunk. He belched loudly, spit constantly, complained incessantly, and couldn't string two words together without inserting a profanity. In short, Bubba made our visit to the lake completely unpleasant. Eventually he passed out in the back of the boat and we enjoyed the rest of the day.

My opinion of Bubba's character, talent and intelligence could not have been lower. I looked upon him as a total loser. A dimwit who would never amount to anything.

At the end of the day, Tony drove Sue and Bubba home first. When we arrived at their home, Bubba was awake and somewhat sober. Sue asked Tony to come inside and see the new dress she'd bought. Then she turned to Bubba and said, "Why don't you show Robert your chickens?"

We walked around to the back of the house and Bubba pointed toward a miniature barn. It was the cutest little building I'd ever seen: gambrel roof, little windows, bright colors, and lots of lacy gingerbread all around.

"Where'd you get this?" I asked.

"I built it," replied Bubba.

"From a kit?" I asked.

"No, I built it after my grandfather's barn."

For the first time that day, I was impressed by Bubba. When we went inside, the first thing I saw was a display case full of blue ribbons. Dozens of them. These were first place awards from around the country that Bubba had won for his chickens. Then he started showing me his chickens and telling me about them. Suddenly the cussing and complaining Bubba became eloquent.

Wisdom in the Weirdest Places

As we walked around the barn he showed me more than 50 of the most beautiful and exotic looking birds I'd ever seen. Unusual looking birds that I would never have known were chickens. These were not birds for eating or laying eggs – these were prize show chickens.

He explained to me that chickens originated in the jungles of Asia. He told me how he bred and raised them. What he did to make their plumage bright, colorful and plentiful. I was amazed by the extent of his knowledge and I listened eagerly to everything he said. He spoke with an enthusiasm and energy that I could not have imagined earlier. The difference was that I had entered his real world. The world he loved and was excited about. Here was his hobby, but he was so motivated by it that it brought out the very best in him.

I learned a big lesson that day. I'd always heard my teachers say, "Don't judge a book by its cover," but until then I had not witnessed the truth of that proverb. I decided then and there that I would never judge another person completely by my first impression. That if time and opportunity allowed, I would look further, deeper.

When you discover someone's passion, you have discovered what motivates them. And, that is the key to communicating with them in the most productive way possible.

Question for discussion or continued thought:

Have you met anyone recently who might deserve a second look or chance?

Robert Evans Wilson, Jr.

Mmmm... the Way You Move Me

Music plucks your emotions like a guitar string

"Oh, sometimes I get a good feeling, yeah I get a feeling that I never never never knew I had before, no no I get a good feeling, yeah."

Those words are an Etta James gospel lyric which has been enhanced by a hard driving guitar and a Rap beat to form the musical framework of Flo Rida's top ten hit single *Good Feeling*. It is the perfect song to get me pumped up in the morning.

Hey hey... baby, baby... rama lama ding dong... yeah, yeah, yeah... music moves us. When I was a teenager, if the song *Radar Love* by Golden Earring came on the radio while I was driving I would find myself pressing a little harder on the gas pedal. Ram Jam's *Black Betty*, Steppenwolf's *Born to be Wild*, and probably a dozen other songs had the same effect. Somehow I managed to avoid getting a speeding ticket. Call it *Luck*.

Sometimes we simply can't help but be moved by music. I love the scene from the movie *Easy A* where Emma Stone gets a musical greeting card from her grandmother that plays the song *Pocketful of Sunshine* by Natasha Bedingfield. Upon opening the card, she proclaims it to be "the worst song ever," then spends the weekend playing it over and over again - dancing and singing along - until she wears out the battery.

I get it, some songs just make me want to move my body... or as they used to say on *American Bandstand*, "It's got a good beat and you can dance to it." Right! Who cares about the lyrics, anyway? OK, sometimes the lyrics of songs I enjoy really annoy me. Perhaps I should've said, "Who listens to the words anyway?" On the other hand, you can't sing along if you don't learn the words. I suppose it depends on the mood you're in. I once heard someone say, "When you're in a good mood, you listen to the music; when you're in a bad mood, you listen to the lyrics."

Music, however, is very personal. What moves me may not move you. Bon Jovi's *It's My Life* makes me feel like I can conquer the world. In fact, music has helped conquer the world... or at least motivated rebellion. In the 1980s, the desire for Western pop music helped bring down the *Iron Curtain* and end the Soviet Union's rule over Eastern Europe.

Wisdom in the Weirdest Places

Patriotic songs and national anthems can be very potent motivators. One of the most memorable scenes in the movie *Casablanca* is when the "Occupied" French citizens sing *La Marseillaise* to drown out the "Occupying" German soldiers singing *Die Wacht am Rhein* in Rick's cafe.

Some music is intentionally designed to pump us up (think of the Rocky movie theme songs *Gonna Fly Now* and *Eye of the Tiger*), and there are songs we use to celebrate, such as *We Are the Champions* by Queen.

Music is so powerful that we revere the people who deliver it. We give musicians - Frank Sinatra, Elvis Presley, and Michael Jackson to name a few - our highest esteem above politicians, actors, and sports stars. We love them for the wonderful feelings they give us. And, what kid has not dreamed of being a rock star?

They have that power over us because, as playwright William Congreve, said in 1697, "Music hath charms to soothe a savage breast." (Yes, I got that right... it is frequently misquoted as "beast.")

Research has shown that music can reduce stress and induce complete relaxation. I have my own list of happy songs such as *Lookin' Out My Backdoor* by Creedence Clearwater Revival that I play when I want to pick up my spirits and chill out. Music that makes you happy or pumps you up will also trigger your body to release serotonin which is a neurotransmitter that will elevate your mood.

Music plucks our emotions like a guitar string. Love, sorrow, pride or anger there is a melody or tune, whether it is classical, jazz, rock, country or rap, that will enhance those feelings. It is so powerful in touching us, that it is second only to smell in generating memories. In a flood of detail, we will recall a specific event or person when we hear a certain song.

Music motivates us in so many ways... but you already knew that.

Question for discussion or continued thought:

What music gets you in the mood for work, play, or romance?

Made in the USA
Charleston, SC
06 December 2014